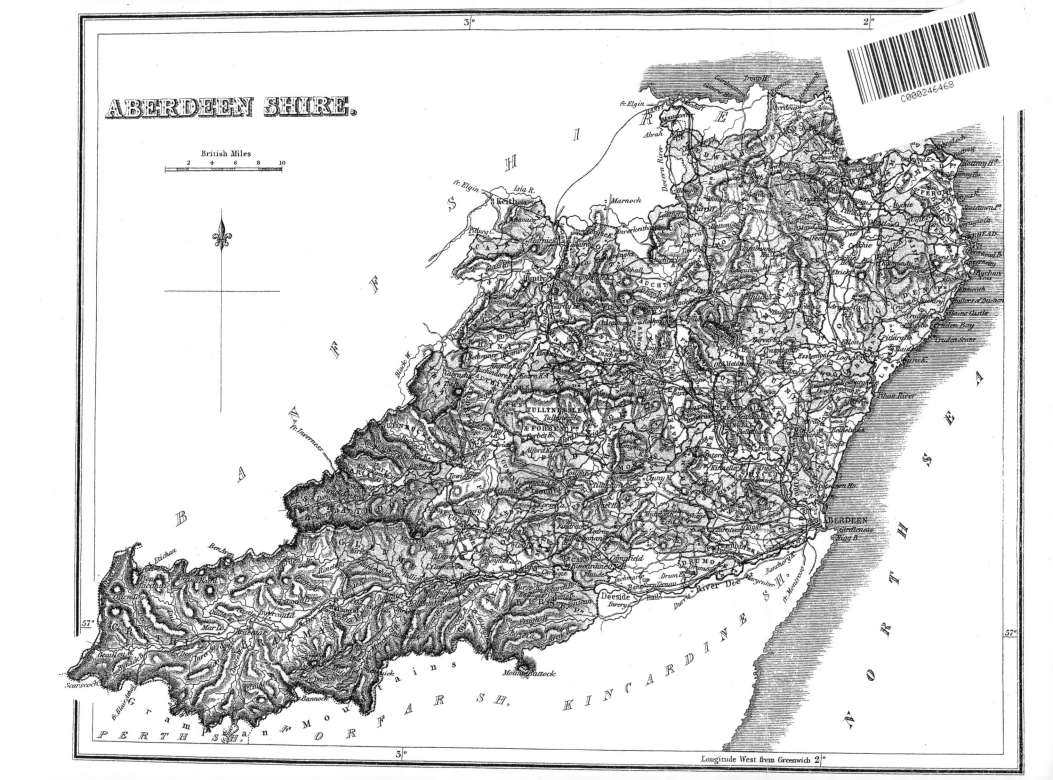

ABERDEEN SHIRE.

British Miles
2 4 6 8 10

3°

2°

NORTH SEA

ABERDEEN

Deeside

KINCARDINE SH.

FORFAR SH.

PERTH SH.

Grampian Mountains

Longitude West from Greenwich 2°

57°

Children Of The Manse

Growing Up In Victorian Aberdeenshire

Alice Smith, at the age of 19, after leaving Frankfurt

CHILDREN OF THE MANSE:

GROWING UP IN VICTORIAN ABERDEENSHIRE

By ALICE THIELE SMITH

Edited by Astrid Hess and Gordon K. Booth

THE BELLFIELD PRESS

© 2004 Astrid Hess and Gordon K. Booth

Cover design by Jennifer Littlejohn, St Margaret's School, Edinburgh.

Family Tree design by Sheena Blackhall, Aberdeen

ISBN 0 9526554 7 0

First published in 2004 by The Bellfield Press, an imprint of GKB Enterprises, 4 Bellfield Terrace, Edinburgh. EH15 2BJ.

Printed by SK Printing, 3 Midtown of Barras, Stonehaven, Kincardineshire.

Price £7.99

A CIP record for this book is available from the British Library

CONTENTS

LIST OF ILLUSTRATIONS

ACKNOWLEDGEMENTS

Our sincere gratitude is due to several academic institutions and to numerous individuals. Amongst the latter in particular are Prof. William Johnstone, Emeritus Professor of Hebrew at Aberdeen University, and Prof. Robert Segal, Professor of Religious Studies at Lancaster University. Both retain a deep interest in the life and work of William Robertson Smith and offered ready assistance to the editors of this very non-academic work. Much is owed also to our respective spouses, Rüdiger and Martha, whose patience and encouragement over many months has been of inestimable value. We are indebted to the Rev. John Cook, Church of Scotland minister in the Howe of Alford, who willingly guided us around the historical sites there, and to Mrs Julia Hayes, current owner of the manse of Keig, who most hospitably gave us access to the house and garden. Dr Jennifer Melville, curator of Fine Art at Aberdeen Art Gallery, gave us generous access to the paintings by George and Archibald Reid, bequeathed to the Gallery by Alice's sister Isabella, while Mr Craig Ferguson of the National Trust of Scotland was equally kind in allowing us to view the many pictures by James Giles which are to be seen at Haddo House. Mr Alexander Macpherson, great-grandson of the artist, gave us invaluable information about the life of the latter. Not least, we wish to thank all the members of the Thiele family who supported us.

FOREWORD

In her Introduction, Astrid Hess describes the serendipitous way in which the materials for this book came to be discovered in her family archives and how her great-grandmother's memoirs were jointly translated over many months of rewarding but often hard labour. Alice Thiele Smith carefully recorded her memories in late age for the benefit of her grandchildren and the very simplicity of her style is in itself one of the book's attractions. At the same time, it is not claimed that the book is a literal translation throughout or that Alice's exact words are everywhere reproduced. In justification for the occasional editorial liberties taken, we would quote the famous remark of her namesake and contemporary – Lewis Carroll's own Alice – "and what is the use of a book without pictures or conversation?"

Accordingly we have now and then introduced an element of dialogue into Alice's text, based faithfully on the original narrative but supplemented by details drawn from the many letters written by the Smith family members to one another, since these provide a key to the way in which they actually spoke, as well as to the everyday topics that interested them. The family letters, together with her father's account of his early life, have also allowed us to correct a few dates and other details where Alice's memory has failed her. All the illustrations and photographs are reproduced from those remaining in the possession of the family.

At one level Alice's story provides a straightforward account of her girlhood in rural Aberdeenshire during the 1860s and 1870s. As such, it offers a vivid and picturesque description of daily life, with all its ups and downs, within the large household of her father, William Pirie Smith, Free Church minister at Keig and Tough from 1845 to 1881. At a deeper level, however, Alice's story has much more to tell the perceptive reader. While death within the family figures all too painfully often, the sexual development of Alice and her siblings remains, in common with respectable Victorian conventions, a completely taboo subject.

Yet very obvious psychological tensions are traceable throughout the story. In virtually every respect, Alice's brothers are treated quite differently from herself and her sisters, beginning with the all-important issue of their education. Alice's barely concealed frustration on that matter is repeatedly apparent, and her ambitions are continually thwarted, even though she genuinely rejoices in the successes of her brothers, William, George and Charles. She writes of a time when the first moves in the long and often bitter struggle for gender equality were being made in Scotland by women like Sophia Jex-Blake and, though her sympathies with that cause are never made explicit, they lie just below the surface of the text like a constant yet unacknowledged irritant.

For the whole family, the eldest brother, William Robertson Smith, justly typified the finest kind of Victorian achievement, won at great cost through a combination of intellectual prowess, personal endeavour and indomitable struggle in the face of adversity. In Alice's tale, Will's presence as guide, supporter and counsellor is always apparent, yet she and her sisters are inevitably required to fulfil subservient roles. From infancy onwards their common destiny, by virtue of rigorous training and conditioning, is to become competent wives and mothers; and their decidedly limited success in those respects is one of the bittersweet ironies of the book.

G.K.B.

INTRODUCTION

I grew up having no real awareness of my ancestry; nor did I know anything about genealogy. What little I knew about my family background formed a patchwork without any definite pattern. As a child, I had of course heard lots of different personal and place-names mentioned but had no sense of how these were connected to my own existence. Besides, there were only a very few family members who seemed willing to speak about my forebears. Luckily, that all changed when the book project began in earnest. From that time on whoever I approached for information or family documents generously offered as much help as they could. So at this point I wish to thank everyone who supported us.

I had always been vaguely conscious that my great-grandmother, Alice Thiele, came from Scotland, that she had travelled to Germany to complete her education, had married a German and had remained there for the rest of her life. I knew that there had been a famous brother and that they were said to have come from a very "pious" family. Various names, like Nellie, Lucy, George and Will, were bandied about but at first no one made any effort to explain how they were related or what stories lay behind those individuals. My own mother and her four siblings showed not the least curiosity about their ancestry – a state of affairs due mainly to my grandfather's military-style attempts to drill them all into memorising their family tree, beating them harshly if they failed instantly to identify their "noble ancestry"! And so it came about that in the end all his children reacted by rejecting such obsessional family pride.

During my grandfather's lifetime it became virtually obligatory in Germany to demonstrate and indeed prove one's Aryan descent, so he fanatically hoarded the family records, far more than was necessary, amassed them into albums and issued orders that everything relating to the family should be handed down from eldest son to next eldest, in strict succession. If the latter had no male descendants, all this documentation was to go to the next "worthy" male family member. Grandfather William started this process by sending the whole mass of material to his eldest son William who had emigrated to Canada soon after World War II. But all the accompanying instructions quickly cured William junior of any natural inclination to find out more about his family history. Even his own children and his brother Martin showed no interest at that time. So after some years, William sent the parcel off to Spain where his sister Ruth, my mother, was living. I cannot say whether she did much with the papers beyond giving them a cursory glance but she did at least make a brief visit to Scotland where she found some of the places where the Smith family had lived. And so the door was opened slightly.

Then my mother died suddenly and about a year later a very large cardboard box containing all the available family records and documents was handed over to me. At that time I was still busily at work as a midwife and there was very little time for me to do more than take a quick look at the masses of photographs, letters and hand-written memoirs. Yet even then I felt a strange quiver of excitement. Though at first I had no idea what I could or should do with all this material, I soon realised that within all the meaningless jumble of names and dates there lay a wealth of fascinating history, often touching, sometimes thrilling, and always enlightening. Don't people say that life itself tells the best stories?

In 1998 I went to Scotland for the first time. Some former school friends had invited me to join them on holiday and so four of us girls set off together. I fell in love with the country instantly. Though it was October and both the climate and the landscape were by then typically autumnal, Scotland immediately became for me the quintessential land of open spaces, fresh air and friendly people – a place where one could be alone without ever feeling lonesome. We visited Aberdeen and its art gallery, where some of the paintings of my Scots forefathers were said to be housed. But my hopes of seeing them were dashed on that occasion since none of them was on display. However, we did find our way to the small village of Keig, located the parish church and explored the graveyard with its Smith family tombstones. It was a first tentative step.

The following year I repeated the journey, this time with my husband, Rüdiger. Naturally we went back to the art gallery in Aberdeen and this time we were more fortunate. Although we still didn't actually view the family paintings, we met one of the curators, Jennifer Melville, who knew at once what we were talking about. I had brought some old photographs, which gave credence to our halting explanations, and Jennifer began to speak about the Smith family – and especially about my great-grandmother's brother, William Robertson Smith – with such enthusiasm that by and by I realised that there really *was* something important behind all the fuss my grandfather had made about his family history.

Jennifer recommended several books for us to read and showed us a copy of the diary kept by William and his friend, the painter Sir George Reid, during a visit to the Continent in 1876 when both men had journeyed through Germany, Belgium and the Netherlands. And it had been on that occasion that my great-grandmother, Alice, and her sister Lucy, were taken to Frankfurt-on-Main to complete their education. Jennifer then told us that as recently as 1994 an international conference had been held in Aberdeen to commemorate the centenary of William Robertson Smith's death. We agreed to stay in touch and I was assured that whenever I had a question I should simply ask her! So it was Jennifer Melville who really gave me the first impetus to start properly with my family project, as I called it. I now felt certain that this would prove a worthwhile challenge.

Alice's memoirs were of course far more accessible and immediately interesting to me than the complex life and work of her famous brother. She had been an inveterate writer all her grown life but always in German, having married Hans Thiele in 1883. Indeed Alice had mastered the language so well that she was able to give tuition in German to children. There was nothing spectacular in her writings – they were all written explicitly for her five children. However, I eventually came across a real treasure in the shape of three hand-written brown exercise books, describing the life of her Scottish family during her childhood and youth. After I had read these several times it became my firm intention to revise and edit these small manuscript documents, together with an account by Alice's father of his early life and education.

Any family history is like a river. Its origins lie in countless small burns fed by the rain and distant mountain springs, all feeding into one another and becoming increasingly interconnected until eventually they form one great stream. Looking backwards we can see that multiplicity of sources, while ahead we can only guess at the river's future course. Those were my feelings as I became immersed more and more deeply in the various branches of the family. Then in spring of 2002, while carrying out research on the internet, I had an unexpected surprise: on one inconspicuous web site I found a complete doctoral thesis about William Robertson Smith, eminent Hebrew scholar, editor of the ninth edition of the Encyclopaedia Britannica and pioneer of biblical criticism in Britain. I wrote to the author, Gordon Booth, and had an answer by return. We were both delighted for Gordon had previously been unable to trace any living descendants of Robertson Smith's family. From then on the correspondence grew in scale and frequency until, rather like my river image, it became a flood. I told him about my project and he confessed that he had cherished the idea of writing a short popular biography about WRS, but had found a scarcity of material on Smith's early life. So it seemed natural to pool resources and work together, beginning with Alice's reminiscences of her strict Victorian upbringing within a large family at the Free Church Manse at Keig.

Along with my cousin, I planned yet another visit to Scotland – being warmly welcomed on this occasion by a hitherto unknown branch of the family who were descendants of the Scottish painter James Giles. Gordon and his wife had also invited us to be their guests in Aberdeen and so we spent three wonderful days discovering all the places associated with the Smith family, their homes in Keig and Aberdeen, the churchyards where their mortal remains had found a last resting place, and the various memorials to Robertson Smith, not least the fine stained glass window in King's College Chapel. And of course we constantly discussed our main topic: how to incorporate Alice's memoirs in a book.

The first difficulty was that Alice's extensive notes were all written in German. I had typed these out and smoothed the text but now all this material had to be translated into tolerably good English. After some hilarious disasters using language translation software, I decided to rely on my own skills and sent the results bit by bit via email to Gordon, who revised the text again and again until it read more naturally. And whatever I lacked in knowledge about Scottish culture or church history in the 19th century, he was able to tell me or could find out at Aberdeen University's Queen Mother Library.

Where Alice had left unintentional gaps or had assumed knowledge on the part of the original readers, we took the liberty of supplying additional details from a range of sources available to us. Her brother William's correspondence with family members, some in my own or my family's possession, some at Cambridge University Library, proved invaluable; in addition there were other very useful documents and photographs in the family archives. Otherwise our guiding principle was always to avoid introducing any fictional element. Curiously enough, I ended up writing almost as fluently in English as Alice had written in German.

My great-great-grandfather, William Pirie Smith, and his wife, Jane Robertson, had eleven children altogether, of whom Alice, born on April 27, 1858, was the ninth. In 1845, shortly after the great Disruption of 1843 within the Scottish Church, her father had given up his comfortable post of head teacher at the West End Academy in Aberdeen to become the first Free Church minister in the rural Aberdeenshire parish of Keig and Tough. The parish lies within beautiful, gently rolling countryside west of Aberdeen, and the village of Keig itself lies close by the river Don, spanned there by one of Telford's finest bridges. The Free Church and its manse lay a good mile or more south of the village, and were conveniently near Whitehouse, a small station on the Great North of Scotland Railway's branch line to Alford, opened in the very year of Alice's birth. Behind the manse, Alice's favourite hill, Cairn William, rises up from the fertile Howe of Alford and she vividly describes the view from its summit of the snow-capped Cairngorm mountains to the west and the North Sea to the east. The manse itself was quite isolated, yet for the Smith children it was a wonderfully peaceful environment in which to grow up, and Alice's love of the surrounding garden is very evident throughout her memoir.

In the thirteen months preceding Alice's birth, her mother Jane had lost two children. In March 1857 a boy was stillborn and in the following October her four year old daughter Eliza died. We can only guess how Jane must have felt during her subsequent pregnancy. As Alice's tale unfolds, death becomes an ever-present feature of life at the manse.

Within the family, the children fell into three groups by age and all were educated at home. The three eldest, Mary Jane, William and George, were the intellectual stars. All highly gifted, they were an especial joy for their father who placed the highest expectations on them. From an early age they were accepted by the parents as equal partners in family discussions. For the younger ones though, they were to be unattainable examples. In the middle came the two sisters, Ellen and Isabella. Both were devoted to their household duties in the manse, perhaps partly through temperament, but also by reason of their mother's uncompromising training. Ellen was talented, outgoing and capable, Isabella very shy and reserved, totally without academic pretensions yet expert in the role of housekeeper. And then came the four youngest: Charles, Alice, Lucy and Herbert. As she tells us, Alice's first conscious memories begin with Bertie's birth.

To complement Alice's picture of the Smith family we have incorporated another hitherto unknown manuscript memoir, this time by the father, William Pirie Smith, and written down by Lucy and Alice at his dictation in the late 1870s. Very formal and antiquated in style, it is in complete contrast to Alice's writing but well illustrates how a gifted yet impoverished young Scotsman could achieve academic distinction through the kind of dogged persistence and self-help then being advocated in the works of Samuel Smiles. Alice's father writes with great solemnity and at times with a degree of complacency yet without intrusive piety. Unconsciously too, he betrays many of the personality traits which his daughter Alice very candidly describes – in particular his nervousness and obsessive drive for achievement.

Now let both daughter and father speak for themselves!

A.H.

PART ONE

BEGINNINGS

My first sure memory is of one cold and stormy February day in 1862. I was not quite four years old and was seated in the manse nursery beside my sister Lucy, who was seventeen months younger. I was aware that something strange and momentous was happening all around in the house but what it was all about I couldn't begin to guess. At length the maid came in and, taking each of us by the hand, led us gently into our parents's big bedroom where by the flickering firelight I saw our mother lying.

"Sit down on the floor, both of you," was all she said; then all at once a small white bundle was placed in my lap.

"Hold him just for a minute," said Mother in a weak voice. "That's your new wee brother, my dears."

This then was Herbert – Bertie as we all called him afterwards – who was to be the very last of my parents' eleven children. Father was minister of the Free Church at Keig, a small village in Aberdeenshire, and it was to prove quite a struggle for him to bring up that large brood on his small stipend, though he always remarked philosophically, "If the Lord blesses us wi' bairns, He surely will provide for them." And so it seemed to happen.

Soon the big wooden cradle where we had all lain, one after the other, was brought back into the nursery. It was broad but low and we would all take turns to rock it gently with out feet. A strong knitted band attached to wooden knobs at each side made quite sure that Bertie couldn't fall out and so I was set to rock the new baby in his cradle. That was great fun at first but the rest of the family seemed to be kept so busy at their work that I quickly grew bored and came to feel that "minding Bertie" was a chore that came my way all too often. There were so many other more interesting things to do.

Herbert's christening in Father's little church where we had all in turn been baptised was naturally a great event for the whole Free Kirk congregation, who turned out in force for the occasion, all eager to know what the Doctor's latest bairn was to be called. The visiting preacher, however, so mumbled the poor child's name that most of the folk in the pews failed to make it out at all, especially as it was so completely unfamiliar to people more accustomed to respectable Old Testament names. Father used to say later that the name Herbert was looked on with great disapproval by many of his small flock. He was sure they would have been much better pleased if Bertie had been named Amos, Elijah or Daniel.

I have only scattered memories from around that time – sharp little images of us younger children playing in the field at the front of the kirk and my brother Charlie running round and round in circles, still dressed in a striped pinafore though almost four years my senior. By then the two oldest boys, Will and George, were already students at Aberdeen University, while Mary Jane, the oldest of us all, was housekeeping for them, and Bella was at school in the city. So apart from Charlie and baby Herbert, we were all girls at that time in the manse: myself, Lucy and Ellen, whom we all called Nellie. One little brother was stillborn a year before my own birth and another sister, Eliza, had died just six months later at the age of four. Lizzie had been a beautiful and kind-hearted little child and Mother found it very hard to accept her death, blaming the doctor at first for failing to treat her illness properly. But Lizzie had in fact suffered from hydrocephalus and nothing could have saved her. So there had already been much illness and bereavement in the home; perhaps that is why I cannot remember a time when either of my parents was not grey-haired.

With such a wide age range in the family, we naturally separated into different groups. There were the older ones, Mary Jane, William and George, who now and then took part in our games or showed us what to do, but who always seemed to me grown up and therefore to be held in great respect. Will in particular took immense care of us little ones, watching over our development and giving advice to our parents. Both Mother and Father trusted him implicitly and relied on his judgement as they grew older.

We all shared our toys but my favourites were a doll and cradle given specially to me, I think, by my parents on my third birthday. Home-made by Father, the cradle was a perfect replica of the big family one, right down to the wooden knobs and cord for rocking it by hand. So very precious did it become that I took it with me to Germany where it has stayed throughout my life. Though it became riddled with woodworm, my granddaughter Elizabeth loved to play with it endlessly as a child.

Of course we had a whole family of dolls to play with, most of them handed down as heirlooms from our parents and grandparents. The oldest ones were very battered and some were incredibly ugly, their egg-shaped heads, carved out of wooden blocks, being the only solid part. Legs, arms and the rest of their bodies were of stuffed fabric and all the limbs were crudely pinned on with bits of bent wire. For eyes there were indented blobs of black sealing wax and a single streak of red marked each doll's mouth. Modern children would be horrified by them, I'm sure, but we loved them all dearly and played happily for hours with our large family. The very oldest dolls in fact became our favourites, even though we were often presented with smart new wax dolls by relatives, friends and former maids.

Apart from the dolls I had relatively few playthings: just

a paint box, a very useful bottle of gum and, of course, my own special cradle. That shortage of toys didn't bother me in the least since we had the freedom of a big garden to play in, as well as the woods beyond.

All of us had home-made stilts for walking on outside – in fact, in those days long before children had bicycles, we considered our stilts to be the only *proper* way of getting around the garden. And in winter time we had a sledge that the older boys had made for themselves long before. For skipping, any spare piece of rope we could lay our hands on would do, though later Nellie brought us proper skipping ropes with real wooden handles back from Germany. We made up other games to play in the garden or else learned them from our older brothers and sisters when they came home at holidays. Will taught us one very special game called croquet that fascinated us: but it was considered slightly dangerous at first and we could only play it when either he or Father was there to keep a careful eye on us.

* * * *

Memories of childhood, like pictures, need to be set in a frame. For me, that frame is the home we lived in – the small manse set all by itself in its lush green surroundings. There was no other house nearby and our nearest neighbour, a small tenant farmer, lived about ten minutes' walk away. From the road, a short driveway led past the drystane dyke through the garden and up to the manse. On the other side of the road lay fields and scattered rows of trees marking the field boundaries. The church itself was set in its own grassy plot, separated from the manse by our fruit garden and the outbuildings: hen-house, cowshed and barn. Beside the church were stables for the convenience of parishioners who came to the kirk on Sundays by horse and cart.

The whole garden was enclosed on its other three sides by a beech hedge of breathtaking beauty and I can still feel how my heart leapt for joy whenever I looked out of the nursery window on a fine spring morning and saw all the trees freshly dressed in green, with the cherry blossom already out and the lilac bushes about to burst into bloom. After a long, harsh winter the whole world seemed to suddenly to be miraculously reborn with incredible beauty.

Behind our beech hedge, wooded slopes rose steadily upwards. There were no dense conifer plantations in those days, only rough moorland dotted with deciduous trees and clumps of pine that overhung pretty fern-fringed dells. Beyond the tree line, there was heather of all kinds – cross-leaved heath, bell heather and ling in profusion – turning the hilltops in autumn to a deep purple. The tiny blood-red blaeberries ripened in August and we knew exactly where to find all the best bushes. Two specially tall, straight Douglas fir trees that grew on the north side of the garden hedge we named His Highness and Her Highness. The boys would climb recklessly almost to the top of these, to the ruin of their breeches and the despair of our mother.

Five minutes' walk brought us to some boggy ground that we had to cross by a couple of planks and then, just beyond, Cairn William heaved up its great bulk, the rough and slippery scree slopes harbouring a marvellous display of spring flowers – white anemones, blue violets and brilliant yellow broom, as well as masses of wild Scottish primroses.

We were good friends with one tenant farmer living on our side of Cairn William. He and his family struggled to cultivate a few patches of miserably thin soil there, just sufficient arable land to yield oats and some turnips to feed a single horse and to give his two or three scraggy cows some chance of surviving the winter. Besides a few hens, those pitiful resources were all the couple had to bring up at least ten children! We always enjoyed visiting the family but Mother would only let us go when there was money enough to buy butter or eggs from them, since she was all to well aware how poor the family was. Even so, the farmer's wife never failed to give each of us a big glass of creamy milk and a large "piece" spread with butter and jam.

Nobody else lived on the western side of Cairn William. As we youngsters grew bigger and stronger, we were allowed to venture further up its slopes. At first the pine trees grew quite thickly, their lichen-encrusted branches hanging over us so menacingly that I always felt a bit scared. It didn't take long to reach the tree limit and then we plunged into knee-high heather that was hard going for a small girl like me. I would plod on gamely all the same and at last we would reach the summit, exhausted but proud of ourselves. In fine clear weather, we then looked over a magnificent panorama.

Far to the east, a thin line of blue showed us where the North Sea lay. Away to the west we could easily see the high, snow-capped peaks of the Cairngorms, while southward, beyond the Howe of Alford, stretched the long uneven mass of the Grampian mountains gradually dipping down towards the sea. Closest to us, and north-east of where we stood, rose Cairn William's bigger brother, Bennachie, with its rugged Mither Tap, separated from us by the River Don in its deep valley.

For a long time it was my heartfelt desire to climb right to the top of Bennachie but only the big boys were allowed to go so far and my wish was fated never to be granted. Our parents judged the expedition too risky for the younger ones and by the time I had grown old enough to walk that far, Father had grown obsessively anxious about his children's welfare. Outwardly, he simply asserted that such long expeditions were quite unsuitable for young ladies.

Even on Cairn William, I was only allowed to go to the very top escorted by one or more of the older children. Will in particular was always willing to accompany me as I struggled awkwardly through the heather, giving me a helping tug of the hand now and then and showing me how to jump from one tussock to the other. That was great fun, I remember, for both of us.

Once, I remember, we caught a young hare; another day I managed to catch a weasel all by myself, though it gave me a nasty bite through the leather gloves I was wearing. At the first house we reached, I handed it over and was greatly praised for being a *braw wee lass* that had got rid of *yon chicken-thievin' futterat* (weasel). I sorely wanted to take it home as a trophy but the dominie from the parish school, who just happened to be there for some reason, pocketed the dead beast without a word and walked off. Maybe he wanted to use it for a lesson in biology but I was absolutely furious at his high-handed conduct and went around for days after, seething with indignation and resentment – though far too shy of course to protest openly.

* * * *

Until I fell in love with the beauty of the surrounding countryside, the garden meant everything to me. After moving into the newly-built manse in 1848, Father had designed the whole garden by himself and then planted every tree and shrub in it. Two tall, slender silver birch trees that we called the Gatekeepers stood, one either side of the driveway entrance like sentries, and the drive itself curved gently upwards from the road to the front door, where there was turning space just big enough for a dogcart. The front garden was laid out in rhododendron and thuja bushes, white and purple lilac, and holly trees, as well as laurel and juniper that Mother made good use of for various culinary and medicinal purposes.

On stone plinths at each side of the front door were two big metal urns, always filled in summer with flowers. These had been a gift brought all the way from Gibraltar by a rather eccentric sea captain who had been a favourite of both my parents. In earlier years he must have visited the manse often because one bedroom was always known as The Captain's Room. From the few times we met, I remember him as a massive, strong old fellow with huge hands, his party piece being to march across the sitting-room and back with Bertie standing upright on one of his outstretched palms, much to our delight and wonderment.

The Captain would always bring Mother a present from the countries he had visited. One gift was a white, beautifully embroidered Kashmir scarf that Mother wore on very special occasions; another was a pair of ivory-handled lacquered Chinese boxes decorated with delicately painted feathers. The Captain's first two wives had died mysteriously leaving him childless, but one day a letter arrived at the manse, announcing that he was about to marry for the third time – this time a widow with four children.

"My heart rejoices again at the prospect of marriage," he wrote.

But both my parents shook their heads in dismay. Mother tut-tutted and Father declared solemnly, "No good will come of this."

As it happened, that was the last letter they ever had from him. He had been a fur trader in the heyday of sailing ships but those days were rapidly coming to an end. Rumour reached us, however, that he soon left his third wife, who had shrewishly nagged him into shaving his beard off.

Back to my subject – the garden! Our lawn at the rear of the house was bordered by several large beds in which grew potatoes, other vegetables and strawberries. There were several apple trees that blossomed lavishly in May yet for some reason always bore poor crops of fruit. Our wild gean trees flowered prolifically and went on to produce masses of small bitter cherries which the birds always ate before we could harvest them. We did have one cultivated cherry tree next to the hedge but it rarely bore any fruit, perhaps because the ground there was so poor. Once only I remember coming back from a seaside holiday to find it covered with cherries: alas, before we could pick any of them they had been gobbled up not only by the birds but also by a pair of red squirrels that had cunningly built their dray there. We were all furious about that but quite powerless to do anything, though some of us muttered, "Why doesn't Father get a shotgun!"

One garden in the neighbourhood, however, did have a fine cherry tree that fruited well. It belonged to an elderly bachelor who had a reputation for being decidedly cantankerous, especially towards children. Luckily though, he seemed to have a soft spot for us girls, very possibly just because we were "the Manse children" but maybe also because we were so obviously just as fond of the countryside as he was. He visited Father and Mother regularly, always dressed immaculately in his Sunday suit complete with gold watch and chain, and would take tea very formally with us all. In turn, we children always found some excuse for visiting him at cherry time. He was often out, driving around the country roads in his rickety gig, but whenever we were lucky enough to find him at home we would diplomatically steer the conversation to our real purpose.

"How are the cherries coming on this year, sir?"

"Well enough," he would grunt in reply. Then without fail we would be quite sure of getting a basketful of fruit from his tree.

For me, the flowerbeds and gooseberries bushes were the most important and precious features of the garden. Earliest to appear were the Christmas roses that Mother picked even when the snow was still lying inches deep on the ground. After that came a succession of spring flowers: snowdrops and dense clumps of crocus; then narcissus, grape hyacinths, violets and lungwort. These were followed in turn by all the summer and autumn blooms. Even in December Father would manage to bring Mother a fresh spray from our monthly rose. But I must admit that it was the gooseberries that captivated us most. We had literally dozens of these bushes, all heavily laden every year and seemingly never growing old. There were so many varieties too: early and late yellow gooseberries; green and red ones; smooth and hairy ones – and the biggest of all, called the Phoenix.

Gooseberries were the one fruit that we were allowed to pick freely from the garden – though only when we were judged old enough to know how much was good for us! The youngest children were strictly rationed to a certain number, from six to twenty at any one time, depending on our ages. Father, I believe, had worked out the proportions mathemathically. So we all eagerly longed to reach the stage when we would be sufficiently grown-up to take as many as we pleased. But inevitably the day would always arrive every summer when I simply could not face any more gooseberries! That happened to all of us girls and it was a complete mystery to me how the boys always seemed able to polish off as many as they wanted.

In fact, they would start eating them before meals, saying, "Gooseberries are perfect for whetting the appetite, you know."

Then, to our horror and amazement they would rush straight back to the bushes afterwards – "Just to fill up the empty spaces," as they always said.

And the supply seemed never-ending. Baskets of gooseberries and blackcurrants were regularly sent off by carrier to our parents' old friends in Aberdeen, while anyone from the parish who wanted fruit could bring a basket and freely pick their own. Right through August and September the great gooseberry orgy lasted, ending in grand style with our annual Sunday School picnic.

For this important annual event, the younger children turned up at three o'clock, accompanied by their mothers, while the bigger ones arrived an hour later. First we gave them soft buttered rolls with jam and cups of tea in the open air, then they played games that Lucy and I organised for them in the garden or the surrounding woods. At six o'clock we gathered them all together so that Father could solemnly address them on the need for gratitude towards God's bounty, after which they were given as many gooseberries as they could manage to eat from a laundry-basket filled to the brim with the fruit we had picked earlier. Lucy and I were always stiff and sore for days after all our physical exertions at the picnic.

As I've said, our apples were forever a disappointment because of the poor soil. Nevertheless we each had our own special apple tree and mine grew close against the wash-house wall, grudgingly yielding a meagre crop of medium-sized apples each year – probably never more than a dozen. Naturally they weren't for me to eat alone since all the fruits of the earth had to be shared equitably amongst the whole family. I do remember one year though when two of the trees each bore an unexpectedly fine crop of succulent rosy-yellow apples – so many that we had to make storage space for them in the cupboards and wardrobe drawers. Then in winter-time our suppertime bread and cheese was supplemented to my great delight with mouth-watering slices of apple.

On the south-facing wall of the manse was our solitary pear tree, a delicately flavoured jargonelle. It bore very few pears though and finally gave up producing any at all, whereupon Father announced that as the tree was thirty years old the boys should chop it down forthwith. We were still more upset when Father told them to remove our two birch trees at the front since they also had grown too old and were, in his view, dangerously weak. I simpy couldn't understand how Father could make the boys do such a thing – hadn't he planted and nourished them himself, like every other bush and tree in our garden? Didn't he always treat every growing thing there as if it were a personal friend? I simply couldn't fathom his attitude. However, there was some compensation. Charlie, who was the family expert in woodworking, made fine hoops out of birch for the croquet game that Will had taught us all.

Masses of tangled ivy clambered up the sides of the manse walls, side by side with several rambling roses. Traditional Scotch roses grew also on either side of the front door and their white flowers would fill the air with fragrance on still, mild summer evenings, especially after a shower of rain. The whole garden sloped gently up from the road, the manse set right in the middle, surrounded by flowerbeds, with the beech hedge and woodlands beyond. Each of us had special responsibility for one bed, where we could plant whatever we wanted – so I had my own special plot of land that was a source of pure joy to me as a child. When very young I naturally had only a very small patch to cultivate but later I was allowed to take charge of a fairly large piece of waste ground and with Charlie's help managed to transform it.

One or two fine old Scots pine trees still stood in the garden. They had been there before the manse was built but the roots got in the ways of the other plants and so the Kirk Session eventually agreed to have them removed, much to Mother's distress though not to Father's. Our two big Douglas fir trees, however, survived for a long time at the back of the garden and the cool dark space they enclosed was always known as "The Shady Bower" – a marvellous spot in hot weather to spend a free hour or so curled up with a book or simply daydreaming.

All kinds of birds made their nests in our trees and hedges: blackbirds with their greenish eggs, thrushes with their blue speckled ones, yellowhammers, hedge sparrows and lots of others. At the back of the house, we had our own children's playground that we called "Grissand", probably from the grey sand that lay in heaps there. We would enjoy puzzling Father's visiting students by announcing, "Let's all go and play at Grissand". Two of the paths also had special names. The one from our front door to the Church was known naturally as Church Walk; and the door to the hen-house was called, unsurprisingly, "Henswalk". And one secluded corner of the garden, for some reason that I never quite discovered, was always spoken of as Bachelor's Corner.

FATHER

How can I possibly describe either of my parents to you so that you see them as vividly as I still do? Hard as I try, the result always seems quite inadequate.

Father had a finely-shaped head, long white locks and a neatly trimmed beard. With his black skullcap on, he looked, so friends said, just like Dürer's portrait of Erasmus, and certainly he made such a strong impression on one of Will's close acquaintances, the Scottish artist George Reid, that he offered to sketch Father's picture, doing so in the old Flemish style, with a triple likeness on the one canvas: full-face in the centre, profile to the right and half-profile at the left. That was in 1877, when I was seventeen, and I remember our feeling of pride when it was hung in the parlour.

Seeing the finished portrait for the first time, one woman who came to our sewing circle in the manse remarked ingenuously to Mother: "Yon paintin' o' the Doctor looks fair picturesque" – a remark that amused us all greatly.

After thirty years' ministry at Keig, Father had grown quite old in appearance but had become increasingly beloved by his parishioners, who took great satisfaction from his wide reputation as both churchman and teacher. Many years later, William Robertson Nicoll, the eminent son of a neighbouring Free Church minister, wrote that Father's sermons were the only ones he had found worth preserving because of the lasting impression they made on him. Though Father had long been known locally as "the Doctor" – well before his old university conferred the honorary degree of D.D. on him in 1873 – it was a memorable day for us all when our postman unexpectedly handed him the letter bearing the seal of Aberdeen University, telling him of the tribute they wished to bestow.

Mother absolutely glowed with joy. Quite out of character, she hugged Father in front of us all and said, "I always kent you'd get it, William!"

As for the rest of us, we were jubilant and immediately begged for a holiday in celebration of the great event. It was in the following year, I think, that Father sat Lucy and me down in the study one day and announced that we would have a holiday from work. "Instead", he said, "I'll tell you the story of my early life and ye'll tak turns writing it doon."

I should tell you here that both Father and Mother invariably spoke the best of English whenever "in company", while inside the family circle they happily lapsed into the local Doric. Anyhow, this was hardly the kind of holiday that Lucy and I expected but we cheerfully set about writing to his dictation – and our joint manuscript lies before me now. After some weeks, however, he abruptly gave up the project – much to our relief, I must admit.

Reading the manuscript again after the passage of so many years hauntingly calls up his voice to me, with its measured, rather singsong, pulpit delivery and his typically meticulous description of the books he had read and the people who had gradually influenced him to return to learning. Rather than try to tell the whole story myself, I mean to include it in his very own words at the end of these reminiscences. It is still interesting to see how Scottish children were brought up and taught in the days of Father's boyhood – and to find how strong was his desire to obtain a good education.

As his own story makes plain, Father had been an indefatigable worker from his early youth. His own father, a rope-maker whose business failed, disappeared off to North America, leaving his wife completely unsupported to bring up three children on her own in Aberdeen. Though he later asked her to join him, she refused – probably because she distrusted his ability to provide for the family. The eldest child, Father's sister Martha, helped from an early age to sew and the two women eked out a frugal living through dressmaking and needlecraft. Mattie had once been engaged to be married but her fiancé died and so she stayed at home until Granny's death, always very much under her mother's thumb. Father's younger brother George drowned as an infant in Aberdeen Harbour, an event Father could never forget, though he makes no mention of it in his own memoir. Our Granny Smith was sternly Calvinistic in outlook and practice, severe and unbending in spirit yet tirelessly diligent in everything she did. We children were always a little afraid of Granny and on the whole felt relieved that we rarely saw her. Once a year she would pay a visit to the manse along with Aunt Mattie but they would never stay more than a day or two and I confess I never learned to love her.

The last time they came to see us, Granny was in her eighties and I remember how we all trooped down to Whitehouse station to watch out somewhat nervously for her arrival by train from Aberdeen. Mother and Father took Granny and Aunt Mattie into the parlour first and a little later we were allowed in to pay our respects. Then we were presented with yet more painted wooden dolls. By this time Father was able to provide some financial support to Granny and Aunt Martha out of his small stipend and in return they would send an occasional box of his favourite smoked haddock – "Finnan haddies" as they are still called today.

I saw Granny only once after that, when Mother and I went to Aberdeen for a few days. Though very frail, she rose stiffly from her seat at the chimney side and with great deliberation unlocked a kitchen cupboard drawer, slowly withdrew two half-crowns and handed them solemnly to me. Sheer riches! She died in 1866 when I was only eight. Aunt Mattie then came to live with us but soon tired of country life at Keig and wanted back to her friends in the city. I imagine too that she couldn't bear the noise we children made or the hectic bustle of daily life at the manse, because she became increasingly irritable and was forever snapping at us. Anyway, it was handy to have an aunt living in Aberdeen and we visited her quite regularly, knowing that without fail she would present us each with some of her favourite fruit sweets. We knew better, of course, than to ask for them!

From his early childhood, Father had shown a talent for learning and Granny would have dearly liked to send him to the Grammar School, had she only been able to afford it. He himself was determined not to be a burden to her and so left school as soon as possible to become apprenticed to a woodturner. Many, many years later, when we were all on holiday near Elgin, we visited the local museum where the curator happened to have a small lathe in his workshop. Father asked for a bit of wood and to our collective pleasure and admiration created in no time at all a beautiful little spinning top which he then handed over to a delighted Lucy.

Father found no real or lasting satisfaction in such practical work though and began studying by night, struggling to teach himself Latin with the help of old textbooks which he had won as school prizes. Eventually he felt knowledgeable enough to sit the University's Bursary Competition – gaining one of the bursaries available was in those days absolutely essential for any prospective student without independent financial means. These scholarships were only just enough to pay for the lectures and to provide the minimum in terms of board and lodgings. Country students traditionally set off to university in November with a load of potatoes and a sack of oatmeal, returning home at the end of March to help out on the family farm. Over the years we got to know many such talented lads from relatively poor families who went on later to occupy important posts at home and abroad.

As he describes in his own memoir, Father duly became a student at King's College, supplementing his limited means as did so many others in those days by giving private tuition in the evenings. To make up for lost time, he would walk to lectures every day, so he told us, with his nose buried in a textbook. Occasionally, when all our work was done for the day and we were sitting round the fire in Father's study, we could persuade him to talk a little about his early life. I recall him telling us how fearful people were in those days of going out late at night for fear of body-snatchers who plied their awful trade in and around the graveyards. We all got the creeps when he told that story.

Father gained his M.A. in 1838 at the age of twenty-seven and, after a brief spell of teaching at the parish school in Kincardine O'Neil, became a teacher at his old school, by now named the West End Academy, an establishment set up by some of the wealthier city business men and reputed by the 1840s to be the best school in the city. And it was then that he met his future wife – our mother Jane – who was one of the teachers there and daughter of his friend and former teacher, Mr Peter Robertson. From then on, until the end of his life, she was to be Father's constant companion and mainstay.

Mother's father died unexpectedly in December, 1842, and Father himself then became rector of the Academy. People used to say later on that he would have had a great and distinguished career before him in education. And Mother used to remark with a smile, "Aye, he was so clever, he might have been Postmaster General if he'd wanted!" – a remark which impressed us children greatly. Yet things were to turn out very differently. "Man proposes; God disposes," as Father himself would always say. Those were the years leading up to the great Disruption of the Kirk in 1843, when more than half the members of the General Assembly in that year solemnly walked out in protest over the undemocratic practice of appointing ministers to their parishes in accordance with the wishes of local landowners.

My parents had closely followed the course of the long struggle against such patronage, taking the radical and evangelical side with enthusiasm. After the Disruption, however, it soon became obvious that there were not enough Free Kirk ministers to cover every parish in Scotland, especially in country areas, and Father was eventually persuaded to accept the call to serve as minister to the rural parish of Keig and Tough on Donside. Many years later, during a train journey, I struck up conversation with an old lady who remembered chatting to the distinguished Professor of Greek at King's College, Prof. Blackie. "The finest student I ever had," he had said to her, "became a humble country minister in Aberdeenshire. His name was Smith – William Pirie Smith." You can imagine my surprise at that chance remark.

The people of Keig and Tough, however, were at first by no means whole-heartedly in support of the Free Church cause and Father found the going very hard at the start of his ministry, for all that he had the support of many influential Free Church members in Aberdeen itself. As often happened elsewhere, the local landowner (Lord Forbes of Keig) at first refused point-blank to provide land for a church and even objected to Father using a barn which had been offered as a meeting-place by one of the local tenant farmers. So he preached to begin with in the open air, despite being menaced now and then by the formidable presence of Lord Forbes looking haughtily from his open coach. Fortunately the dispute resolved itself fairly amicably in a short time and the building of the new Free Church at Keig was completed in 1846.

Lord Forbes himself stayed mainly in London by that time and his son, who occupied Castle Forbes at Keig, paid several friendly visits to my parents. The old Lord, however, when he did condescend to pay a very rare visit to the manse, would signal his arrival by rapping loudly at the door with his walking stick while at the same time ringing our bell furiously. He did send Father a token present of game during the hunting season, as was his custom towards all the tenants on his land, but he never showed any real warmth – that would have been beneath his aristocratic dignity. On the other hand, Lord Forbes' aunt, who had lived in Germany and Switzerland, quite frequently came to worship at our church and in later days became a good friend.

There was a good deal of bitterness, however, between the Free and Established Churches in most parishes. Both parties were jealous of the membership numbers and became intensely upset if an individual or family defected to the other side. And "mixed" marriages were considered deplorable. Years after the Disruption, one young minister, who had been newly ordained to the established parish church at Keig, went visiting all the families in the area, regardless of church affiliation, and was snubbed by one woman with the remark, "I'll nivver, nivver set fit inbye thon kirk o' yours".

The young man smiled benignly at her and responded, "Come, come, my good woman, we shall surely all be one in the Kingdom of Heaven."

The answer was sharp and instantaneous: "Foo ken ye that, ma loon, fan ye've been yonder nae mair times nor me?"

Church affairs assumed far greater importance in those days and feelings ran very high over what today would seem trivial matters. Religion still lay deep within the soul of the Scottish nation – in rural places at least – and to ignore the accepted rules of church attendance or moral conduct was to risk being shunned in the community. Bitter sectarian disagreements over the finer points of belief were part of the traditional pattern of life in the days of my Scottish childhood, as they had been for generations before. Only with the twentieth century did reunification gradually come about and more liberal attitudes begin to prevail.

* * * *

Our parents' eldest son, William, was the first child to be christened in Father's newly-built Free Church at Keig. He had been born on a Sunday in November, 1846, in a cottage at New Farm which our parents had rented before the manse was completed. Father didn't only act as minister to his people. He gave evening classes for the young men of the parish and arranged for visiting lecturers to come and speak to them. He had purchased a magic lantern for use at those lectures and used to show us slides projected on to a white sheet pinned to the nursery wall. We were all enthralled by this scientific wonder, especially when he showed us pictures of the stars and solar system.

Father also had an "electrical machine" cranked by hand, from which (if we were brave enough to hold the two metal grips) we would be given small yet unpleasant electric shocks. I was much keener on the astronomical slides though and they impressed me so much that I used to lie in bed dreaming of becoming an astronomer when I grew up. Alas, it was of course one of the boys, Charlie, who was to achieve that ambition.

As I've mentioned, I was only three when Will and George both went off to Aberdeen University, accompanied by

Mary Jane – at sixteen the eldest of the family – who was to be the "little housekeeper" in their Aberdeen lodgings. Bella also went with them, attending an Aberdeen school, and I still have a beautiful photograph of the four of them, taken professionally in Aberdeen. All are wearing their best clothes, the two girls dressed in fashionable crinolines. Will was then just turned fifteen, George was not quite fourteen, and both had gained top awards in the Bursary Competition, which meant that they were virtually self-supporting. One uncle – I forget which – showed his admiration by presenting them with a fine new timepiece so that they might get to their classes on time. Having been educated completely at home by Father until then, going to university was their first real experience of the big outside world, yet both boys and Mary Jane, quite unlike Bella, thoroughly enjoyed the experience.

At home in his parish, Father was always ready to help anyone who wanted to learn. He vividly remembered the help and advice he had been given in his youth and so a young man only had to come and talk over his ambitions with Father to be given every assistance, being allowed, if he had the talent, to join in the morning classes at the manse. Some even stayed for meals and Mother would offer them tactful hints on table manners or etiquette generally – advice they were only too glad to have at the time and for which they expressed much gratitude in later days, after having made their way in the world at home and abroad. Others came to us as boarders at the manse in order to get special tuition from Father.

Poor Mother's resources for feeding such large numbers were often very stretched indeed and the fare was extremely plain. She told us that in those early days Father's stipend was so meagre that she often could not make ends meet and so was forced to borrow money at the end of each quarter, though she always paid it back as soon as she could. Oatcakes and porridge were certainly our staple diet at first. However, the modest fees paid by Father's boarding students soon became sufficient to make a real difference to the family finances. Most of these young folk fitted very well into the household and benefited greatly from their tuition by Father, even though he was extremely strict and had no qualms about using his leather strap – the tawse – on any pupil he judged to be careless or slothful.

Father himself was the most diligent of workers until his physical health declined and he began to find difficulty in making lengthy visits on foot to the parishioners. When that happened, people would willingly offer to take him by horse and cart on his pastoral duties, especially when a sick person needed his ministrations urgently. Otherwise we four girls often visited on his behalf when we were old enough – a very pleasant task which helped maintain the close tie between manse and parish.

At home, there was still much for Father to attend to. He would always write out his Sabbath sermons in full and these were kept secure in a large, locked wooden box in his study. Naturally he never took his sermon manuscript into the pulpit – that would have been quite unacceptable to a Free Church congregation! Sometimes he would brood for days over his theme for the forthcoming Sunday. Like the apostle Paul, he believed most earnestly that the Holy Spirit should breathe inspiration into his preaching. One Sunday, I remember, just before the service was due to begin, Father was restlessly pacing up and down because he simply could not think what to say. Only when he actually stepped into the pulpit did the words come to him; and then he preached with such sincere passion and authority that the congregation was enthralled.

Sunday morning worship lasted for two hours in those

days, yet no one seemed to wish it otherwise. After that came Sunday School for the children. Mother was in charge but we girls each took a group once we were considered responsible enough to do so. A couple of men also helped with the older boys' classes and Father looked in from time to time. Sunday School, conducted by some of the elders, was never a great success, however, and the result was always the same – attendance would start well in the autumn but rapidly dwindled because the teaching was far too dry and uninteresting for small children. Father himself took the Bible Class, which catered for those young men and girls preparing for communicant membership of the Kirk. There was no actual sacrament of Confirmation: those who had attended the preparatory classes simply went along to Communion with their parents once they were judged fit and ready to do so. Making their profession of faith in this fashion by attendance at the Lord's Table was considered far too solemn a matter to warrant any kind of celebration or gift. For my part, I loved the Bible study with Father and so felt quite resentful when told to take charge of the youngest Sunday School group, even though that eventually gave me a good deal of pleasure.

Throughout the week, Father undertook all the teaching of the boys themselves, though he did eventually give me some instruction in Maths and Latin. On top of all those duties there was of course the big garden to look after, a task he relished for as long as his health allowed. In the course of time he became less and less able to cope with that work, becoming, in quite an odd way, nervously agitated over the welfare of his plants – I recall him saying, for instance, that whenever he had been pruning the gooseberry bushes he would then suffer dreadful nightmares about being attacked by thorns.

Father's small library remained a constant source of

pleasure to him and for a country minister he came to have a well-stocked library, even although he never could afford to acquire all the books he wanted. He subscribed moreover to many of the academic and theological journals of the day and so was well able to keep abreast of the latest ideas. It was said that one of his colleagues in the Alford presbytery, Dr Harry Nicoll, was an even more obsessive book collector, so that his children were almost faced with starvation. On the other hand, they inherited a remarkably grand library on his death.

Father, however, always put the family's needs before his own personal interests and in the early days would do no more than buy an occasional second-hand book in Aberdeen. These were mainly German theological works and, despite never having been taught German, he set himself to learn the language on his own and continued that task until he was well over sixty. The problem of being unable to afford such luxuries was eventually solved once Will began to visit Germany and could afford to bring the latest publications back home for Father.

When the children were all young and at home, extravagance in such matters was not to be thought of; yet in Father's study there stood a very fine edition of the Greek Old Testament (the Septuagint) in two thick volumes, which were to be handled by no one else. It was a great puzzle to me therefore that they were always spoken of as *"Bertie's Septuagint"*. Many years later Mother explained the mystery to me.

"You see," she said "Papa desperately wanted a really fine edition of the Greek Old Testament but knew he certainly couldn't afford the expense. After Herbert's birth, though, a good friend in Aberdeen gave him a generous amount of money to buy a christening gift for the wee bairn. Papa shut himself away in his study and spent hours worrying (and doubtless praying) about the matter but in the end reached a decision that satisfied his conscience. The books would belong to the baby but Papa would have the use of them meantime! And that's why they're called *Bertie's Septuagint*. Puir Bertie! He'll never make a Greek scholar."

Mathematics, however, were Father's greatest passion and all his maths textbooks stood ranged on either side of the big Bible that was used for daily worship, morning and evening. The study of mathematics always seemed, at one and the same time, to exert a stimulating and a calming effect on Father. Certainly, as he grew older, he spent more and more of his leisure time in the pursuit of solutions to the most complicated maths problems. Will and George used to boast, perhaps tongue in cheek, that Father was heading steadily towards the solution of some complex problem or proof that had until now defeated all the greatest minds. Both the eldest boys were themselves brilliant at mathematics and the family talent was inherited by my own daughter Jeannie, who would always sit down at her maths work with a sign of satisfaction, saying, "It's so wonderful to be able to do this!"

As I've said, Father was always sensitive to the needs of others and could easily be moved to tears by the misfortunes of his parishioners. That meant of course that all the wandering beggars who came around knew they could safely rely on getting a few coppers from him. If they went round to the back door around dinnertime, they were also sure of having a bowl of soup and some bread or oat cake from Mother. Some of them naturally would cunningly call at both doors. However, as a Free Kirk minister, Father was very severe in his condemnation of Sin. Anyone in the parish who fell from grace and sinned openly knew full well that he or she would have to come before him expressing sincere penitence and then be faced with a lengthly moral lecture before they stood any chance of being admitted once more to the Lord's Table at Communion time.

We children likewise knew all about Father's severity. It was bad enough to be reprimanded or punished by Mother – not that she was ever harsh in her treatment of us but because we were always so dreadfully conscience-stricken by her slightest reproof. Her words would bite indelibly into our hearts. But it was still worse on the very rare occasions when she sent one of us to Father for punishment. The leather tawse with its fringed end hung menacingly behind his chair and, though it was seldom if ever used to punish any of the girls, still the very sight of it was quite enough to terrify us.

I remember only one actual instance when Mother sent me in disgrace to see Father and I have no idea now what the misdeed was. Probably I had been stubborn in some way – for that was *my* besetting sin. What remains etched in my mind is that slow, reluctant walk to his study and the sense of utter humiliation that filled me. I think we younger children were all very much in awe of Father and more than a little afraid of him. Certainly he had grown more tetchy with age and found it difficult to tolerate the kind of racket that children make when playing together. So as much as possible we kept out of his way by inhabiting the nursery which was situated upstairs, above the kitchen and at the far end of the house from the study where he worked and taught. Downstairs there had to be total silence and only those who were members of his class were allowed into the study. Will told us that it had all been very different when he and George were young and before the years of grief came to take their toll of both parents. In those days, he said, Father had been the most cheerful and communicative of teachers – a true comrade in learning to them.

Altogether, Father spent just over thirty-five years in his

country parish at Keig and Tough – from 1845 to 1881. For the last few years of that ministry, he had an assistant and indeed could have remained in the post until his death; but he knew that would not be right and moved to Aberdeen with a small pension. There we stayed for some years in a flat in Skene Place, before moving to Fountainhall Road in 1889, when Will could afford to buy a larger house for the family. Eventually, following a stroke, Father became an invalid and gradually grew too weak to walk unaided. He died contentedly in February, 1890.

By that time I was married and living in Germany but during my last visit to Aberdeen, when he knew he would not be long spared, Father's parting words to me were, "All in all, Alice my dear, I've been very lucky". I was at least somewhat cheered by knowing that Mother, Lucy and Bella had a comfortable home.

MOTHER

Dear, kind Mother! How much we all owed to her. She was forever Father's loyal, understanding wife, the cleverest, most economical of housewives, able to feed and clothe us on the slenderest of means. Not only that, she was the minister's helpmeet who knew of every need in the parish and was always ready to lend a helping hand. Nearly forty years after Father's retirement in 1881, I went back to Keig in 1919 and met local folk who still remembered Mother with gratitude and affection. One old lady told me how she had learned all her dressmaking skills from Mother – just as we girls had done. Simply her presence in the house was enough to bring us comfort and strength in the most difficult of times.

At the same time, our mother Jane was a typical Scotswoman of her time, rarely giving expression to her true feelings and maintaining an outward air of equanimity that belied the many trials, physical and emotional, that she must have gone through. I well remembered the time in 1878 when Will was setting off for a tour of Egypt and the Middle East that was to last for several months. We were all sitting in the living-room waiting for the cab to call when Mother suddenly disappeared and I eventually found her standing in tears at the back door. That was typical of her stoical determination never to show her feelings in front of the family. She came back inside with me but even when Will was actually setting off a few minutes later, there was, apart from her cheerful farewell smile, not the flicker of emotion to be seen on her face.

Her childhood had been a hard one. She was born in 1821 but her own mother, Isabella, sister of the notable Scottish artist James Giles, died young, leaving three small girls of whom she was the eldest. Her father, Peter Robertson, quickly remarried but his choice of stepmother was an unfortunate one, at least so far as the girls were concerned. The new wife showed scant affection for the step-children and life became even harder. Indeed my mother felt so miserable at one point that she went to stay with her grandmother, Jean Giles, for several months. However, as you know, Mother became a teacher in due course and readily obtained a post in her father's school, the West End Academy.

Admission to teaching was a simpler business in those days and her practical skills in needlework and housewifery were quite sufficient to serve as qualifications. When Peter himself died in 1843, the stepmother, who had become a milliner after her husband's death, expected the eldest daughter to clean the house, mend the clothes and work in the shop after a hard day's teaching. Mother was never strong and it was little wonder that she began to feel no better than a slave in that situation – so Father's proposal of marriage must have come, I suspect, as a promise of deliverance.

I must not forget to tell you that Mother herself came from an interesting family. Her grandfather, James Robertson, started out in life as a handloom weaver but became one of the first Congregational ministers in Scotland. He and his wife Agnes moved to the Aberdeenshire village of Stuartfield in the parish of New Deer, where he was ordained in 1802, ministered there for thirty years, married twice again and eventually emigrated to America in 1832 with part of his large family. My brother Will had numerous friends at New Deer who would tell us how great-grandfather James was still remembered there in the 1870s with great affection by some of the older villagers. After four years in Vermont, old James was called to a Congregational church at Sherbrooke in Canada where he acquired a considerable reputation and ministered until his death. Mother's aunts, Margaret and Mary, received a better education than most Scottish girls of their day, attending the Holyoke Ladies' Seminary in South Hadley, where they were classmates of the famous poet Emily Dickinson. Mary actually became principal of Sherbrooke Seminary for a short time before she married a Free Church Minister. Their fourth son became the famous Canadian writer of adventure-books, Charles Gordon, "Ralph Connor", while Margaret, after fifteen years of teaching, went on to become a best-selling novelist, often drawing on the vivid memories of her early life in Scotland.

As I said, my maternal grandmother, Isabella, was the sister of James Giles, a famous Scottish landscape painter. Mother took us once to the graveyard of St Machar's Cathedral in Aberdeen, where he and her parents are buried, and pointed out with considerable pride the ornate and imposing family tombstone.

"Uncle James designed it himself," she said. "It's from my side of the family, ye ken, that you girls inherit what drawing ability you have. James had a hard youth but his talents were recognised by no less a person than Lord Aberdeen at Haddo House – the Lord Aberdeen who was Prime Minister at the time of the Crimean War. Anyway, James had painted some fine pictures of the deer on the estate and his lordship invited him to plan out the policies there, so that there would be what he called 'a fine vista' to look over from the drawing room windows."

"Was he pleased with the result?" I asked.

"Deed he was," said Mother emphatically. "One thing led to another. His lordship commissioned him to paint all the great Aberdeenshire castles and one of these was the old

Balmoral Castle. And it was seeing that picture that made Queen Victoria and Prince Albert fall in love with the place. Of course they had their own castle, the new Balmoral, built in its place. Yet they aye expressed their gratitude to James for having given them the idea of living there!"

* * * *

But back to our life in Keig. Mother's sewing skills were truly exceptional and her speciality was needlepoint lace, the creation of fine lace patterns, working on a design pricked out on linen or paper which was later cut away. Even in her old age at Aberdeen, friends would flock to her for advice on different types of stitching and when she herself came across a new style of embroidery she only had to examine it closely to pick up the technique instantly.

She was adept too in all kinds of delicate craft work, fashioning ornamental baskets and tiny toy cradles, for example, out of walnut shells beautifully decorated inside and out with lace trimmings. Making clothes for all our dolls was of course a skill of Mother's which we especially prized. Since her hands were never idle for a moment, it was easy for her to turn out masses of handiwork for church sales – and these were always the first to be snapped up from the craft stall. Once, I remember, she made a whole selection of feather pen wipers, each one with a different kind of doll at the other end – a soot-black chimney sweep complete with brush and rope; a fishwife with her laden creel (the fish made out of tinfoil) looking just as we saw them on the quayside at holiday times; a peasant girl; a grand lady and many more.

Married life was no bed of roses for Mother though, even at the outset, because Father had felt it his bounden duty to provide for his own mother and his sister Mattie, who moved in at once to stay with the young couple at their home in Aberdeen. This was very hard indeed on my mother Jane because both women were constantly demanding and patronising towards her. Her physical health even then was poor and at times she felt she had moved out of the frying pan only to find herself in the fire.

Mother's curls, for instance, were her pride and joy, yet her mother-in-law insisted they were "maist unladylike" and should always be modestly covered by a matronly bonnet. For the sake of domestic peace, Mother yielded to the demand but managed to assert her independence by deliberately letting a few curls peep out provocatively. At least she always did so, so she told us later, until Mary Jane, the first of her children, became old enough to tug those curls so mercilessly that Mother kept them firmly out of sight ever after. Fortunately these particular trials came to an end when Father received his call to the Free Church charge at Keig in 1845. The offer that his mother and sister should accompany them to the country was turned down point blank, as I think he expected.

People often wondered why Father, as a newly-married man, gave up his secure and prosperous post as headmaster to embark on a life of relative privation, ministering to a tiny Free Kirk congregation within a part of the country that was predominantly "Moderate" in church matters and therefore unenthusiastic about the Disruption. Knowing him as I did, I'm certain Father must have agonised long and hard over the offer but ultimately concluded it was his duty to obey what was, for him, a God-given call. At the same time I imagine that he was influenced – perhaps unconsciously – by the knowledge that only such a radical break from city life would truly liberate Jane and himself from domination by his relatives. Perhaps that explains why he handed over virtually all his life savings to his mother before leaving for Keig.

Whenever I give free rein to my memory, I can vividly picture all the old familiar scenes within the manse. I see Mother, for instance, seated on her low nursing chair, peacefully breast-feeding Bertie. By then she will already have made her daily round of the whole house and given out orders to the maid and kitchen lass as well as to the children. Only then does she allow herself to sit down, crooning softly while busily occupied with her sewing or knitting. Mostly she sings psalms because those are so central a part of our daily life – and the only kind of sung worship countenanced by the Free Kirk.

Each morning we would all sing three or four verses from one of the psalms; and each evening we would do likewise. Only when Nellie was old enough to play the piano did we have an accompaniment. Little by little, we had to learn by heart all one hundred and fifty metrical psalms from the Scottish Psalter, and every Sunday morning we would crowd round Mother, jostling to be first to recite the six verses we had learned that week. There was never the least dislike of this task and the youngest ones were always desperate to be considered old enough to start learning the psalms too.

I always liked to start memorising the week's verses the Sunday before, while lying in bed first thing in the morning. Then I would go over them every day when working in the garden or out walking; and if we girls were promenading together we would all join in, singing inharmoniously at the top of our voices. Luckily, the country roads were nearly always deserted so there was no one to take offence at the cacophony we must have made. Most of all we loved the triumphal psalms, like the twenty-fourth:

The earth belongs unto the Lord,
And all that it contains . . .

and especially the verses which were always sung at Communion:

Ye gates, lift up your heads; ye doors,
Doors that do last for aye,
Be lifted up, that so the King
Of glory enter may.

Most of all it was the fine tune of this psalm that appealed to us. We loved singing the "Old Hundredth" too (and lived up to its words):

All people that on earth do dwell,
Sing to the Lord with cheerful voice.
Him serve with mirth, his praise forth tell,
Come ye before him and rejoice.

I see Mother seated on her round, hard-backed chair on one side of the fireplace, with Father opposite. Her Bible lies on the mantelpiece above her head and the big work basket sits at her feet. Even when we had visitors, she would continue to sew because the business of making and mending the family's clothes was never-ending. Long practice enabled her to work automatically and visitors were naturally given her undivided attention.

Again, I see her sitting with my first reading-book in her hands while I stand at her side, a small child with blue eyes and long fair hair, struggling to master this new skill. Those first lessons were short – not more than half an hour – and I was soon free to run outside and play. But gradually the amount of work increased, with simple arithmetic being added to the daily routine. My fifth birthday brought a special honour because I was then allowed to take part in the Bible readings during the twice-daily family worship. To begin with, my efforts must have been very slow and faltering, and I'm sure I stumbled badly over the more difficult names in the Old Testament. Even so, I felt proud and satisfied with my performance.

Everyone in the household was present at family worship, servants and boarding scholars included. First we sang part of a psalm; then came the Bible reading: Old Testament during morning worship, New Testament in the evening. Each person there would read one verse in turn, always beginning with the youngest literate member of the family. After the oldest brother or sister had read, it was the turn of Father's boarders; then came the servants and finally Mother, followed by Father. Woe betide any child who lost the place or forgot his turn. Father would give the miserable culprit a withering glare or, even worse, sternly rebuke the guilty person by name!

Each year we began the Old Testament at the Book of Genesis and, with only a few omissions, read the whole Bible through. I found parts terribly tedious and some chapters, like those in Leviticus, extremely puzzling (and of course they were never explained) but it did ensure that we all became thoroughly familiar with the biblical text. At the conclusion, we all knelt down while Father prayed. Then it was bedtime for the younger children. The older ones had the privilege of staying up longer but even so I was twelve years old before being allowed to go to bed any later than nine o'clock. Twilit summer evenings spent out in the garden were glorious; but just as pleasant were winter evenings spent in the living-room, reading or playing games of chess at the big table by the soft glow of our paraffin lamp, with Father watching and advising all the while.

"Tak' yon rook, lass! Can ye no see that's the move!" he would cry, becoming ever more frustrated at our slowness.

Mother was small and always frail, as I remember. Her own youth had been physically demanding and after Bertie's birth she had severe health problems which made her a semi-invalid. I believe it was then that Bella, who had never relished book learning, developed her real talents and became Mother's mainstay in the running of the manse.

The treatment prescribed by our doctor for Mother was of the most painful kind, plasters coated with Spanish fly being applied to her breast daily over a number of years. These produced large blisters which had to be lanced and which never healed up properly since the process was repeated, night and morning, over and over again. Mother would dab soothing ointment on the spot with a soft cloth but I am sure her sufferings must have been intense. I never heard her complain, however, and the whole procedure was so much a daily feature of our lives that we little ones thought nothing of it at all. I know though that I could still instantly recognise the small round cardboard boxes which held the plasters.

Our parents' north-facing bedroom was a cold, draughty place and why the guest bedroom – far cosier and sunnier – was never used when she was ill remains a mystery to me. Possibly no one thought of the idea but more probably the very best room had to be kept immaculate for visiting clergy, no matter how rarely they came to the manse. Only George was occasionally allowed to take his books there so that he could study in perfect peace. Yet I recall how thoughtful Mother could be whenever the needs of other people had to be considered. Once at least she arranged for a bed and mattress to be sent to a sick parishioner so that a night's rest might be enjoyed in some comfort.

It was Mother essentially who brought all the girls up, though Father was always there in the background as the ultimate figure of authority. There was never disagreement between them – none at least that we ever witnessed. We all knew which parent we ought to approach in particular matters; once the issue was settled there was never any question of appealing to the other parent.

Very rarely, Mother would hesitate and say, "I'll talk to Papa about that. Wait until tomorrow."

And occasionally Father would remark, "Umph! I must have a word about that with Mamma first".

From the very earliest age we were all trained rigorously in the path of Duty, a road to be pursued steadfastly by means of those three guiding lights: Truth, Love and Diligence. Mother had a store of favourite sayings which she trotted out on all appropriate occasions. If ever we said, "I can't do that, Mamma," she would automatically respond, "If at first you don't succeed, try, try, try again!" And so on. Once I came to her with a bad tear in my pinafore.

"Well, Alice," she said, "find a needle and thread and mend it."

I explained that I had tried, truly I had, but simply couldn't manage. I declared that the material was too thick – but I knew in my heart that I really wanted out to play.

Needless to say, the inexorable reply was, "If at first . . ." So there was nothing for it but to follow her rule, which always worked out in the end. In this way all the daughters of the manse learned to knit and sew from an early age. I picture myself in the nursery, busily hunched over a small bag that I was sewing quite eagerly because I looked forward to being praised when it was finished. However, I had big, clumsy hands and could never make the stitches sufficiently small and neat to come up to Mother's standards.

She would say, "Quite good, Alice, but the stitches are lying over each other – just there, see; and here they're much too close to one other". But poor Lucy was even worse off than me. Her sewing was so slack that the stitches didn't hold at all.

We were all regularly warned to be scrupulously honest in everything, no matter how trivial, and another of Mother's favourite sayings was: "He that thieves a peedie preen, syne he'll tak a bigger thing!" I still have qualms about picking up a pin that isn't mine.

Perhaps the moral lessons we learned were over-strict at times, but our consciences were certainly sharpened and that was probably all to the good. Telling the truth was all-important and was a principle firmly instilled by both parents: "There's no such thing as a small lie," they'd caution us, wagging a finger and quoting the Biblical injunction: "Let your yea be yea; and your nay, nay; lest ye fall into condemnation."

We had few opportunities to play along with other children in the scattered community at Keig and our position as daughters of the manse didn't allow us in any case to mix freely. Of course we used to be formally invited to special events like christenings; and sometimes we went with our parents to take tea with a church elder and his family. When we were young, we thought those occasions very dull indeed because we had no freedom to play inside, but sometimes we managed to slip out into the garden or farmyard with our host's children. Then we would take pleasure in examining all the cattle and poultry.

Mostly though we were only too glad that Father was always anxious to make an early departure from such visits, which he probably found every bit as uncomfortable as we did. Even if we had successfully disappeared into the fields somewhere, he and Mother would take their leave without us – but always on the strictest condition that we must be home by seven in the evening. On fine summer days that seemed harsh, but if we happened to be the least bit late Father would work himself into a genuine state of agitation and we would arrive home to find him pacing nervously up and down the manse drive looking out for our return.

He was even worse if Mother had been invited out by herself, as happened now and again, or if she had gone alone by train to Aberdeen for the day. Once she had been asked to tea by the wife of the biggest tenant farmer in the district. Hours before it grew dark, Father became fretfully restless and was soon beside himself with worry. This quite irrational anxiety was only eased when he caught sight of the pony-cart bringing her home in good time. Maybe his fearfulness had something to do with the death by drowning in Aberdeen harbour of his younger brother George.

So, while we were good friends with nearly everyone in the parish, we were never on really intimate terms with anyone and had no close childhood friendships outwith the family. Later on, our parents did make an attempt to compensate for this and invited two nice girls from respectable farming families nearby to come along to the manse every morning so that they could be taught with us by Mother.

Winters at Keig in those days seemed to last for ever, with lots of rain and snow. We all suffered from health problems of one kind or another and were often forbidden to go outside in bad weather for fear of "catching our deaths". So we had to make the best of it and find things to occupy us inside. It was wonderful though what Mother could think up to entertain us on those long, dreary days in the nursery. She would say, "If you're all good, I'll show you something special this afternoon," and then we would all be agog with anticipation.

Once, for example, she came upstairs with a small pan containing alum which she had melted. In a day or two we all had our own multi-coloured crystal gardens growing in little bowls on the nursery windowsill. Another time she showed us how to drip the yolk of an egg gently into a glass of water. The strangely mysterious shapes into which the yellow yolk gradually turned as the sunbeams played on it were meant to predict one's fate and fortune. Though a common enough ploy with young and old alike in the countryside, Father would unquestionably have denounced the practice as "satanic superstition". For once, therefore, Mother warned us to keep it a secret from him.

Illness did bring some compensations because only then were we given special treats. Once, I remember, when most of us were seriously unwell with whooping cough, Father arrived back from a Presbytery meeting with a new ball for each of us – his justification being that some exercise with the balls would ease our coughing. So then we had immense fun playing ball games incessantly and seeing which one of us could bounce her ball for longest without dropping it. None of us though could manage to juggle with two balls as Father could.

During yet another bout of illness, when both Lucy and I were in bed, Mother made each of us a little basket out of cardboard and coloured paper. She decorated Lucy's basket with fancy patterns made from grains of corn carefully glued on. Mine she covered with small shells and seaweed gathered from rock pools while we had been at the seaside and then preserved – she had shown us how to wash the seaweed in fresh water and then lay it gently to dry on sheets of blotting paper.

One day an old Jewish pedlar from Germany arrived at our door selling pictures. This was such an unusual event that Lucy and I were allowed to choose one each. I picked a colour print of Martin Luther, who was a hero of mine. Will was at home at the time and when we called him in, he embarked on a lengthy discussion in German, much to the old fellow's delight since my eldest brother was the first person he had met in Aberdeenshire who could speak his language. Both prints were then hung in the nursery after Mother had made frames for them out of broad strips of wood from the local joiner, decorated with fir cones scales arranged very neatly to form a rectangular border. Inside that background she made still more elaborate patterns using fruit pips, the kernels and husks of beechnut, larch cones and acorns. By helping her, we passed the long winter evenings happily.

Her handicraft versatility was inexhaustible. I recall Mother making the most wonderful leaf skeletons for instance. The leaves were first soaked in a dish of rainwater, then carefully set in a sheltered spot where they could be in full sunlight. When the leaves had grown soft and half rotten, they were picked up very delicately, washed clean and laid out on a pillow. Then came the long and tricky task of using a brush to remove everything from the leaves except for the vein structure. That took much time and infinite patience.

Sometimes Mother used pressed ferns as decoration, placing the fronds on boxes, fixing them with pins and then brushing the surface all over with Indian ink. When the pins were removed and the ferns lifted off, their patterns stood out beautifully clear and white against the black background. She gave me one of those boxes, complete with lock and key, for a birthday present and it became my greatest pride and joy. It even had my name inscribed on it, resplendent with its fern wreath borders. I was forever losing things – especially my penknife – but I never lost that key. More than sixty years on I still keep that box beside me, though my name and the patterns are almost completely worn away by now.

How Mother found the time to do all those things is a mystery. She had to look after us all and make all our clothes by hand. When I was young she had, of course, no sewing-machine and so it was a great day when Will, who always worried about his mother, was at last able to buy her one. Sewing machines were an extreme rarity in rural Aberdeenshire at that time and we were all desperately keen to see how it worked. Mother took some time however to learn what was an entirely new technique and we all impatiently yearned to have our turn at operating this miracle of science.

Every one of our garments had to last as long as possible and when the outside of a coat, skirt or blouse became worn or frayed it had to be carefully remade, the inside being turned out to make the material look as good as new. That meant unpicking all the stitching by hand, using only a needle – a job delegated as usual to the girls. That was wearisome work but at least we did it only for short spells, in between more interesting occupations. Sometimes the seams had already been pulled apart so that we only had to check the hems carefully and pick out the loose threads. If Mother was working with really heavy material, she would get one of us to support the other end for her. Then I would sit and admire her deftness. She had the most beautiful, white, well-shaped hands and fingers. All of us girls were jealous of those hands because not one had inherited from her either their shapeliness or their skill – why, I have no idea.

When the boys came back home from University each year at Easter, it was Mother again who (with some complicated structural advice from Father) organised the erection of a triumphal arch made out of plaited evergreens and flowering currant. Then we led them in procession up the drive and under the archway that we jokingly called The Church Door.

Not every such homecoming, however, was to prove a joyful occasion.

1. The Manse of Keig about 1914

2. The United Free Church of Keig early 20th century, now a barn

3. William Pirie Smith, by Sir George Reid, painted in 1877

4. Jane Robertson Smith, by Archibald Reid

5. Will at the age of eight   6. George about fourteen

7. Bella, George, Mary Jane and Will when going to Aberdeen in 1861

8. Nellie about twenty years old

9. Charlie in his twenties

10. Lucy, aged seventeen

11. Bertie, early childhood

HARD TIMES

Back in the 1860s, Scottish boys aiming towards a profession generally went off to university at a younger age than happens today. Studying for an honours degree lasted four years, then as now. The university year was a good deal shorter though, beginning early in November and lasting only until the following Easter, when many of the students went home to help out on the farm, at least in country areas like ours. After achieving a first degree (in those days an M.A. only was on offer, except in medicine) an able young man might then embark on further vocational studies in law or divinity.

My two eldest brother, Will and George, had of course received all their school education at home from Father but in 1861 they both enrolled simultaneously at Aberdeen University, at fifteen and not yet fourteen years of age respectively, each having gained bursaries. The year before had seen the union of the city's two previously independent colleges, Marischal and King's, into a single university. First year students, known as bajans, all wore short red gowns, sometimes with velvet collars – quite medieval in appearance but certainly bright and picturesque in the grey granite streets of Old Aberdeen.

Every autumn, when term began, there followed by long tradition a good-humoured running battle amongst the bajans to snatch each other's gowns, whether by stealth or brute force. A gown torn to shreds except for its collar would then be worn with pride for the rest of the term. A few students though were determined to keep their gowns intact and my two well-brought-up brothers fell into that category. Either way, honour was satisfied.

At the very end of her sons' student days, Mother took all the material from their discarded and worn-out gowns and added it to the great heap of remnants out of which she made rag rugs for the wooden and stone manse floors. In that particular instance she surpassed herself by making a masterpiece out of the red velvet gowns, following an intricate pattern drawn on paper by Will with mathematical precision. We all helped to tear the material into narrow strips, measuring the width exactly with a ruler, while Mother knitted these together into bigger segments using very large needles. All the separate pieces were then laboriously sewn together – very tiring for Mother's hands.

We girls would spend whole afternoons together in the nursery, cheerfully tearing cast-off clothing into strips and stitching them together to make large balls that were then taken off to a local handloom weaver, who duly turned them into carpet runners for the hall and passageways of the manse. They were hardly objects of beauty but served their purpose by making it much more comfortable for our bare feet in winter time. And the stone floor of the hall didn't have to be scrubbed nearly so often either.

I have already told how, in that autumn of 1861, our two eldest sisters, Mary Jane and Isabella, also went off to Aberdeen with the boys. At sixteen, Mary Jane was judged well able to act as housekeeper to them. Bella was only twelve but both girls were allowed to attend a town school. All four stayed in a rented flat with two bedrooms and a living-room. Their meals though were provided by the landlady, as was the custom. I can easily visualise the four of them solemnly bent over their studies of an evening, all so well disciplined that there would be not a sound till work was finished each night at ten o'clock sharp – they had promised their parents never to work beyond that hour. On Saturday nights they allowed themselves some relaxation over a game of chess and the boys also took part regularly in the student debates which were held on a weekday evening. Mary Jane occupied much of her spare time writing both short stories and verse and had hopes of having some of that work published in *Chambers Journal*. Before leaving for Aberdeen, she and the two boys had taken enormous pleasure in producing their own home-made "magazines". One, I remember was *The Iris*; another *The Dandelion*; and yet another was called, more prosaically, *The Weekly Review*. Probably Lucy took them to India and sadly none of these childhood literary productions has survived.

Now and then most of the professors invited their students to an "at home" and both George and Will naturally went along to these evenings. Sundays, however, were wholly given over to church attendance, followed by improving reading at home. Nothing in the nature of light literature was approved of and even going for a recreational walk on the Sabbath was frowned upon. I remember Will saying later how acutely embarrassed he had been in Germany when invited to go for a walk or a meal on Sundays. To some extent our Free Church days of rest were not unlike orthodox Jewish Sabbaths in their strictness and, to me at least, Sundays often seemed interminable. I doubt though if the boys ever found Sundays dull, because they were for ever brimming over with intellectual ideas – it was considered no sin at all by Father for his sons to argue about philosophical or scholarly matters after church service.

At Christmas the two boys and their sisters came home for two weeks' vacation and it was then wonderful to have them back with us. Without the teenagers, the manse could often seem eerily quiet, and their return at vacation times seemed to bring the whole place to life again. The boys held long discussions with Father on the latest ideas in theology or science and were more than willing to join in our children's games with great enthusiasm. The boarders themselves were by then away home and we were once again a complete family, even though the younger ones still had to spend most of their time in the nursery and were only allowed into the living-room at certain set times of the day. But the Christmas holidays inevitably passed all too quickly and on the last day a distinct feeling of gloom would settle on us all.

After two years in Aberdeen, Bella decided not to go back with the three older ones, saying she always felt unwell in the city air. So Mother had a willing and welcome helper in the house from them on. Bella never talked of her stay in Aberdeen but I suspect her real reason for not returning was a wholehearted dislike of all book learning. To the end of her days she remained quite unable to write a proper letter! Maybe her intensely shy, timid personality also made her fearful of mixing with other children in a school setting. She refused point-blank to take part when Father suggested she join some of the lessons in his study. And only once do I remember her leaving home, when surprisingly she paid a visit to some cousins in London, where she saw all the sights, went to the Crystal Palace Exhibition and brought me home two elegantly slim glass vases, one of which I still have.

Bella's strengths lay in her practical abilities. Her efficient management of our large household soon allowed Mother to be relieved of much of the daily work and worry. She was an excellent cook and was in her element baking bread or preserving fruit. The kitchen eventually became her absolute domain and she would barely allow any of us to encroach on what had become hallowed ground for her. Even when I asked Bella to teach me some of her cherished cookery secrets, just before I married, she refused to tolerate my presence in "her" own little empire, the kitchen.

That memory recalls another incident. When I was about eight, Bella was persuaded to stay for a few weeks with a local family that we knew well. She agreed on condition that Lucy accompanied her and as a result I felt quite lonesome. So Mother bought me some pink muslin and showed me how to sew dresses – perfect imitations of our own – for my favourite wooden doll. With tremendous care and effort I completed two simple dresses and became a very proud little doll's mother. But as soon as Bella saw them on her return she couldn't rest until she had laid hands on the leftover material, along with a variety of odd ribbons and bows, begged from our maid. She then proceeded to make a highly ornate dress for Lucy's doll which of course put mine completely in the shade. I was bitterly jealous and never again clothed my doll in what now seemed my miserably poor dress-making effort.

For all that we missed the older ones when they were away, we knew the spring term would soon be over and that they would all be coming home at the start of April for a whole six months with us. And, sure enough, back they would duly arrive, the boys laden with so many finely bound prizes, emblazoned in gold with the University crest, that a new bookcase had to be bought to hold them all. Father and Mother were naturally delighted by their eldest sons' academic success yet were even more pleased that neither seemed to have been unsettled or spoiled by their student life in the city. Our parishioners were almost equally proud to read the papers and find "Dr Smith's loons" figuring at the head of the prize-lists.

In 1863, at the end of their second year at University, there was the same cheerful homecoming, the three youngsters being welcomed again through our triumphal arch at the garden gate. This time, however, both boys seemed rather pale and tired. Mother put it down, she insisted, to "the bad city air" rather than to the strain of studying. William had been a very delicate child when younger and our parents had often feared for his life. It was George, however, who now gave greater cause for concern because he seemed unable to recover his strength and began to cough a great deal. Even I, still just a child of barely five, noticed how anxious both parents had become. They never spoke of their concern to us children but I would hear the servants whispering to each other, "Aye, it'll be the loon's lungs, yon hoast."

George lay listlessly every day on the sofa, very pale except for the unhealthy flush on his cheeks. Then he began to spit blood occasionally. Still nothing was said to us by either parent about George's illness but fearing the worst I kept my eyes and ears open for any scraps of information. The doctor arrived in his little gig, examined George and eventually pronounced him fit to return to University in the autumn. So all seemed back to normal once more. In the following spring, however, we were sent word that he had fallen ill yet again – the diagnosis this time being one of pleurisy. Mother wanted to set off at once for Aberdeen so that she could nurse him but her own health was so poor then that Dr Williamson forbade it decisively.

"Twad be the death of ye, Mistress Smith, an yer ither bairns can ill spare ye!" he stated bluntly.

So Mother capitulated with a heavy heart, in deference to the professional advice of a man we had all grown to love and respect.

Epidemics of all kinds were commonplace in those days and I remember one particularly severe outbreak of diphtheria in the district. There was no hospital out in the country and the patients were nursed at home by family members who all too often succumbed to the infection themselves. Father nevertheless felt it his clear duty to visit all the sick of his parish until one day he was overtaken by Dr Williamson, who demanded to know what he was doing.

"Going my rounds, just as you are," Father answered.

"Bide ye at hame, man. Bide at hame!" said the doctor sharply. "Ye canna help thae dyin folk nane; an waur, ye'll smit yer ain bairns wi't."

"No, no," said Father, "I have my flock's spiritual welfare to attend to, just as you have to see to their physical care."

But Father was no match for his friend, whose will again prevailed on that occasion. I think it was the threat of putting his own family at risk that swayed him.

So when George fell ill, it was Mary Jane who loyally cared for him in Aberdeen. Once fit to travel by train, he came home accompanied by Will and by degrees grew stronger again. But the anxiety over his health remained. Mother's lips would smile as always but her misted eyes betrayed her feelings even to me.

Strangely enough, my few clear recollections of Mary Jane stem only from 1864, when I was six years old. She had been out visiting one of our neighbours and on her return came straight upstairs into the nursery, smartly dressed in a brightly coloured crinoline, very much in the fashion of the day. She had long curls too, just like those of which Mother had been so proud in her youth. All I actually remember of that incident was her insistence on calling her darling Lucy "Fairy"; yet to me that fragmentary memory remained indelible, and ever afterwards Mary Jane stood as some kind of ideal example of womanhood and feminine beauty. Just two months later, she was dead. Throughout her final illness I hadn't been allowed near the sickroom but, just before the end, Mother called me in, saying, "Only a wee minute now, Alice."

In a very weak, tremulous voice, Mary Jane told me that she was now going away to be with God. I was to try, she said, to be a very good child, to obey Mamma and Papa always, to love Jesus and be a ray of sunshine to all the family because they were going to feel sad. Two days later, she died peacefully, having chosen her own epitaph from the seventy-fourth psalm: *Thou shalt guide me with thy counsel, and afterward receive me to glory.* How appropriate that seemed to me for ever after.

A few days later we stood at the nursery windows, peeping out from behind the closed blinds to catch a glimpse of the long funeral procession headed by its black-suited pallbearers. Both parents were grief-stricken yet took comfort in their sure and certain hope of the resurrection to come. They bravely continued therefore with their daily lives and on my next birthday, Mother gave me Mary Jane's beautiful sewing box as a keepsake – and in turn I presented it to my granddaughter Elizabeth on the occasion of her confirmation.

* * * *

Will meantime returned to Aberdeen on his own to complete his M.A. at King's College before embarking on the Divinity course which had been his aim ever since, as a small boy, he had climbed up on a chair and delivered a sermon to the assembled family. This time he lodged with an old, almost blind widow, Mrs McDonald, who had previously entrusted her own son to Father's care and instruction. In turn, she promised faithfully to give Will every maternal attention, much to Mother's relief. The widow's oldest son, Archie, then an aspiring lawyer, became life-long friends with Will, who always had a natural talent for making friendships in spite of his strict and socially limited upbringing.

Apart from his delicate constitution, my oldest brother was

always remarkably short in stature, being barely over five feet tall. For all that, his nature was a tough one and he loved physical exercise – indeed he was foremost in proposing the installation of a gymnasium for students at New College in Edinburgh where the annual subscription was (if I remember correctly) the princely sum of sixpence. To me, Will always seemed mature far beyond his years and Father once wrote of him, "I venture to say that really he was never young in the ordinary sense." He had an intense love of argument and debate, which later was to give him the reputation of being a "controversialist", yet he had an acute sense of justice and right-doing. Mother told the story of how, when very young, he had on one occasion been given some sweets with the advice, "Take one whenever you feel the need". Later on that day, Will seemed unusually ill at ease and, when asked what was wrong, he answered, "I took a sweet when I didn't feel the need."

Father and son were almost of one mind and took great delight in discussing all the scientific and theological issues of the day. After Darwin's epoch-making book on the theory of evolution was published in 1859, the pair of them spent ages debating the consequences for religion of this radical idea. And it was much the same with geology and the great problem about the age of the earth, both of which topics had raised immense questions around the Church's traditional beliefs regarding scriptural accuracy.

Will's last term at Aberdeen University was drawing to its close by the first weeks of March in 1865 and I began to long desperately for his homecoming so that he would chat, tell stories and play games with us as always. But on the first day of his final exams he suddenly felt ill, could hardly put pen to paper and became quite unable to concentrate on the task in front of him. Painfully he struggled home to his lodgings in the teeth of a gale. This time the doctor, an old

Aberdeen acquaintance of Father's, pronounced it a case of severe pneumonia.

Mother was sent for at once and took charge of the battle for Will's life. For days he hovered between life and death. Heartfelt prayers were offered up by his many friends, while gifts of fruit and other delicacies arrived daily at the door, along with expressions of hope for his speedy recovery. In those days the University was a close-knit part of the community and it seemed as if almost everyone in Aberdeen was aware of this young and promising student's dire condition. Both my parents still had numerous friends and acquaintances in the city, from their teaching days at the West End Academy, and all sent messages of sympathy and encouragement. Will's professors called also to express their concern. They spoke of his outstanding achievements and the brilliant future that awaited him. He would, they insisted, gain his degree even if unable to complete the exams. He had been confidently expected moreover to gain the award conferred annually on the most outstanding final year student – the Town Council's gold medal – but that could not be awarded without an examination. Rules were rules. Will must undergo some form of exam, no matter how unorthodox. Might they not sit by his bed and examine him orally?

Poor Mother was placed in a dreadful quandary by this proposal. She asked for a medical opinion and was told the exam could proceed in a few days' time, provided a doctor stayed in the next room while three professors interrogated Will at his bedside. So it went ahead, Mother sitting in fear and trembling beside the doctor, her hands clasped tightly and her lips moving in silent prayer.

It seemed, she told us later, no more than five minutes before there came a knock on the door from inside the bedroom. Mother gasped, thinking Will had collapsed; but instead the three gentlemen, smiling broadly, emerged from the sickroom to announce, "Your son, Mistress Smith, has passed his exam with flying colours, Congratulations! All is well."

Once Will had recovered slightly, he was brought home to the manse, still wearing a hideous respirator over his mouth and nose. That remains one of the many pictures that haunt my mind, like those of Charlie in his pinafore or Mary Jane playing with Lucy in the nursery. The summer passed peacefully, however, and both our eldest brothers became stronger again. It was decided that William should wait a year before going on to his theological studies in Edinburgh. That would give him time to prepare himself adequately and also to try for one or other of the major awards available. George meanwhile seemed to have made a full recovery after his earlier illness and so, accompanied by Will, he was allowed to return to Aberdeen in the autumn of 1865 to complete his degree. As usual, they came home briefly at Christmas and all seemed well.

At the end of March, Mother went off to see her son graduate on "Capping Day" at King's College with its fine old crown-topped tower. Each begowned student solemnly stepped forward to be capped and to receive his parchment roll from the Rector's hand. George had been an especially popular student so that when his turn came there was thunderous applause and great stamping of feet throughout the hall, professors, guests and parents all joining in. Even during lectures, it was said, George used to be "ruffed" in this way by his fellow students whenever he volunteered a particularly brilliant answer in the lecture room.

After the ceremony, George and Mother visited a well-known local bookshop in Old Aberdeen. There they were approached by Professor David Thomson, one of George's most eminent teachers. Giving George a friendly slap on the shoulder, he turned to Mother and said, "You maun tak guid care of this laddie when he goes home. He has worked very hard indeed."

In fact, George had excelled himself, gaining almost every honour and prize open to him and also, like Will the previous year, gaining the Town Council's gold medal for best student of his year. His name was on everyone's lips and we younger children were all as proud as Punch. George himself was quietly modest as ever. There was a happy homecoming and great rejoicing in the parish at the "lad o' pairts" who had grown up in their midst and had brought reflected glory upon them by his achievements. As ever, we had erected the triumphal arch at the Church Walk and eagerly watched out for their arrival at the station. Will now proposed to spend the summer in Germany before starting at the Free Kirk's New College in Edinburgh. He had won prize money for an essay and that would easily cover his travelling expenses. On the other hand, it was George's intention to head for Pembroke College, Cambridge, to study his favourite subject, mathematics. For the time being, both young men were to take things easy for a few weeks. For the whole family it was one of our happiest times. But life for us all was about to take an unexpectedly cruel twist.

One morning I woke up to find a changed atmosphere in the house. There was none of the usual bustle or chatter; no one came to get us up. Everything was quite unnaturally hushed. I crept downstairs to find the maid standing there, exchanging whispered words with the kitchen lass. No one else was to be seen but all too soon I learned what had happened: George had suffered an acute haermorrhage through the night and Dr Williamson was already in the house. Being still so young – this was just before my eighth birthday – it was impossible for me to understand fully what was happening, nor could any of the younger ones. All we knew was that there was some dreadful crisis, but that was enough to weigh me down with anxiety and alarm. All the boarders were sent home immediately and our own lessons stopped abruptly. The bigger children had a multitude of tasks to see to, while all that Charlie, Lucy, Bertie and myself could do was to wander aimlessly in the garden, to and fro, up and down, round and round.

Mother scarcely ever left George's bedside and we caught glimpses of her only when she stepped out of the room to give orders. At mealtimes no one spoke at all and the days seemed endless. We were expected to stay completely out of sight and sound – if possible in the garden, though even there we had been forbidden to make any noise whatsoever. We had no wish to play in any case and a general air of deep misery descended on us all.

To our questions about George's condition, we got only vague, ambiguous replies. In fact, the haemorrhaging recurred only once and some hopes were then expressed for his recovery; but his strength was exhausted and his lungs had been irreparably damaged by tuberculosis. Nevertheless, specialists arrived from Aberdeen and various remedies such as ice packs were applied – all quite ineffectual. Again we were inundated by gifts of what were, to us, unheard-of delicacies, like veal. One day Mother handed each of us some grapes, the very first I had ever tasted.

On the first Sunday after George had fallen ill, we sat together in the living-room while both parents were upstairs with the invalid. Will came in, sat down imposingly on Father's chair, and told us tersely just how serious things were.

"Let's all pray together," he then said, and we all knelt down while he gently and solemnly offered up prayers, first for George, then for our parents and finally for everyone in the family. That seemed to me not only right and proper but the only meaningful action that any of us could take. And it seemed to help, because we had laid the heavy burden on to God in His infinite wisdom. In that household our faith was securely anchored in the love of God and we felt confident of the future, whatever might befall.

Preoccupied as Mother was with George's illness, she could not fail to notice the depressed faces of her usually merry children, who now morosely idled away the hours out in the garden. One day she called our nurse, Betsy, and said, "Take the bairns up the hill behind the moss and let them play there as much as they want."

At first that seemed a wonderful idea and we all trooped off, crossing the marshy ground of the peat moss and clambering up the hill slopes till we were well out of earshot. I remember the scene all too well. Betsy sat down on a boulder and we others scampered off. But it was hopeless. Nothing we did could raise our spirits. I tried a few half-hearted skips and shouted to the others to join in but none of us had any real urge to play. It was quite impossible, I discovered, to become happy to order.

Our hopes for George's recovery grew slimmer as each day passed and Mother no longer even sat down to meals with us. Only when instructed by Dr Williamson to take some rest would she think of leaving her son for a minute and our parents' bed was moved in beside their patient. One morning Mother called me to be with him for a few moments. In a very weak voice, George spoke to me in the familiar way he had always done, then dismissed me with the words, "Cut along now, wee ane. Off wi ye." I went out of the room sobbing bitterly.

Fearfully we little ones sat silent in the nursery. Then a faint sound came from the sickroom: it was George singing one of his favourite paraphrases, that beautiful passage from Hosea:

Longer hath the night of sorrow reign'd;
The dawn shall bring us light;
God shall appear, and we shall rise
With gladness in his sight.

That was a deeply moving experience for each of us, but most of all for our parents. Mother was never able to speak of it and Father only much later, and then always with tears in his eyes. George's death throes were hard, for he fought valiantly but in the end he died very peacefully, feeling himself close to Mary Jane. Early on the very day of my eighth birthday, April 27, 1866, he passed away, just two years after his beloved big sister's death.

Those were very dark days that followed. As the custom was, all the blinds in the house were again lowered and remained so until after George's burial. We still rarely saw anything of either parent even though visitors arrived daily at the manse to pay their last respects. I was freely allowed to go into the room where he lay at rest so peacefully. Though I had been assured there was nothing to fear, I still went in on tiptoes, feeling infinitely scared, and could not bear to look down at the body. On the day of the funeral, George's coffin was carried all the way to the village churchyard by a group of his former fellow-students who had come all the way from Aberdeen and beyond to pay their farewell tribute to him, while the men of the parish turned out, clad as ever on those occasions in their Sabbath suits of black. No women in those days attended a burial, not even the closest relatives. Instead, we all watched discreetly, along with the servants, from behind the window blinds. Mother did appear afterwards, however, to receive the many folk who came back to the manse for refreshment and next day the blinds were drawn up as life very slowly began to return to normal.

Even at the age of eight I felt a bitter sense of waste over George's death. He was such a happy, quick-witted brother, more boyish and less serious in conversation than Will (though every bit as clever) and full of unaffected charm. Unlike Will too, he loved music and singing. Father used to tell us the story of how he had once taken George on a pastoral visit to a farmer's wife. Being shown around the garden as usual, Father had greatly admired certain of the plants.

"Haud on a wee, Doctor," said the wife, "an I'll gie ye ane."

She took her knife and struggled unsuccessfully to dig up the roots. Then father had a go, with no great success.

"Och, bide here till I get a spade," she persisted and despite Father's protestations rushed off in search of one.

George, who could hardly have been much more than four at the time, smiled at his father and whispered conspiratorially, "Women insist!"

* * * *

Just before those sad events occurred, Mother had been busily fashioning two beautiful new dresses for Lucy and me out of some light and colourful woollen material patterned with small blue stars. Brightly coloured clothes of any kind were quite out of the ordinary at the manse and I think Mother had felt stimulated by the fine spring weather and the boys' imminent homecoming. With our girlish love of new things to wear, Lucy and I were absolutely delighted but there had been no opportunity even to try the dresses on. Now, with George's death, that chance had gone for good.

Instead, two dressmakers arrived at the manse, ensconced themselves in the nursery and set to work making mourning dresses for us. Even four year old Bertie was garbed in a smock of funereal black. Our bright dresses were given away to a family of Macgregors who had come down to live here from the Highlands. Mrs Macgregor had been delighted by this gift and thanked Mother profusely.

Several weeks passed and one day Mother remarked that she had never seen the dresses being worn to church by any of the Macgregor girls. "I fear," she said, "that yon Mr Macgregor thinks those dresses unsuitable for his daughters."

"I don't doubt it, Jane," my father said with a rare touch of irony in his voice. "Our Mr Macgregor will not wish his lassies to be tempted into the sin of vanity by clothing them in such frivolities. He is now one of my elders, after all, and a pillar of the Kirk."

Then he added, as if anticipating the hostility which Will was to meet much later from what he called the *Highland horde*: "Aye, Jane, all wordly gear is plain vanity to our friends from the north. They are kittle cattle indeed and like to cause us a peck of trouble."

It was very naughty of us but Lucy and I couldn't help noticing the striking resemblance between Mr Macgregor and a certain black and white cockerel of ours, whose dangling wattles were just like the elder's very prominent ears, and ever after that particular cock was known to us as Old Macgregor. To our genuine surprise, Father was pleasantly amused by this and proceeded to draw our attention to the fact that our little Shetland cow had a head that was the spitting image, so he said, of Dr Begg, a certain eminent and troublesome Free Churchman of the day!

Back to the matter of our clothes. One of Mother's best friends since childhood was married to a wealthy Aberdeen businessman and whenever she came to visit would bring us dress material of excellent quality which cost very little and went far to providing clothes appropriate to their status for four rapidly growing girls. Another well-to-do family in Aberdeen used regularly to send us bundles of cast-off clothing, along with new remnants which, to save Mother's embarrassment, they would say had been picked up for next to nothing at clearance sales. Everything was accepted gratefully and made full use of, with any leftovers being handed out to large and needy families of the parish. It still amazes me how Mother managed so well on Father's small stipend. She would repay the kindness of our Aberdeen friends by sending them a variety of small gifts from our own produce – baskets of fruit in the summer, an occasional hen, a box of fresh eggs, gingerbread or even bunches of flowers.

Much later, Will could afford to bring us the most wonderful lightweight linen dress material from Germany. The first time he did so was certainly a red-letter day for the young ones, all the more so as Nellie, who had been to Germany with him in 1869, had sent us samples beforehand so that we could choose the patterns we liked best. Both Lucy and I at once selected for the same beautiful light blue material. In the early days things had been quite different and we all had had to learn humility. I still remember, during one cold winter, being made to wear an old jacket of Charlie's. That mortified me terribly and I briefly felt a stab of angry resentment towards Mother – but I think her action might well have been intentional, since pride was one of my besetting sins in childhood. Mother always did her best to teach us all never to be ashamed of poverty, only of our own misdeeds.

Father himself fell ill shortly after George's death and was confined to bed for several weeks. If anything, this was beneficial for Mother since it gave her no time to brood and helped her get over those grim days after the bereavement. Then, just as Father was getting back on his feet once more, our eighty-four year old grandmother died. Off went Father to Aberdeen to clear out the small house there and returned to Keig bringing his sister, our Aunt Mattie, to stay. As it was important that she should feel properly "needed", she was put in charge of the three youngest children – me, Lucy and Bertie – while Betsy the nursemaid was discharged. At twelve years of age Charlie was already treated as one of the big boys, while Will, whose visit to Germany was postponed for that year, had begun his studies in Edinburgh, accompanied by Nellie who was to attend school there for the next two years.

Until then we hardly knew our old aunt but had often imagined how wonderful it would be to be cared for all day by someone within the family. The reality turned out to be quite disagreeably otherwise: Mattie was a real old maid, absolutely fixed in her ways and quite unused to dealing with children. When combing my hair, she would tug at it viciously and if I yelled she would snap, "You're far ower feart for yoursel, Alice ma bairn!"

However, she had one weakness which proved some slight consolation for our tribulations. Four times a year she made an expedition to Aberdeen to meet her old friends and to collect the interest from the small capital sum that remained from the money Father had given his mother before he and Mother left for Keig in 1845. Granny had carefully saved it for emergencies and so Mattie had a modest income from which she indulged herself by purchasing enormous quantities of fruit lozenges, mainly for herself but partly, I must admit, for us children. Every day each of us was given one or two sweets and if ever the stock ran out we felt deprived since we very rarely got sweets from any other source. If a visitor did bring some such goodies as a gift, they were put carefully aside by Mother and strictly rationed for very wet days or perhaps as a reward for having done all our duties without fail. Of course we never dreamt of buying sweets ourselves.

Though everyone tried hard to make Aunt Mattie's stay as comfortable as possible – even her sofa was brought from Aberdeen to Keig and lugged upstairs to the nursery – the whole arrangement proved to be a fairly unhappy one and I think every one of us sighed wholeheartedly with relief when, after nearly two years, she demanded to return to Aberdeen where all her cronies lived. We always visited her though on trips to Aberdeen and then she would unfailingly give us a cup of tea with special biscuits from her cupboard. In great old age, she came back to stay with Mother and Bella at Fountainhall Road at the end of the 1880s and there Mother nursed her until her death in 1896.

Aunt Mattie's departure from the manse in 1868, however, finally brought to an end the need for a children's nursemaid. Until then, Lucy, Bertie and I had been known as "the wee anes" or "weans" – an expression I hated – and when indoors we had been more or less confined to the nursery, which doubled as the schoolroom where Mother taught all three of us. Now we enjoyed much great freedom and the nursery became instead "the young lassies' room" for all four sisters, where we sat together, hammering out plans for the day and visions for the future, reading together, working at our tasks and altogether feeling more mature and self-confident.

In August, all four of us would go to gather blaeberries from the hillsides. A pound or two at most of the tiny fruit was all we could expect but then we would buy sugar out of our own pocket money to make blaeberry jelly. In winter, when the baker came on his weekly round from Alford, we would buy rolls for ourselves and feast on "jeelie pieces" in the nursery. That was a very rare treat however and, after Nellie had gone off a second time to Germany with Will in 1871 when I was thirteen, things were never quite the same again. Though she came home after a year abroad, she was engaged to be married; her interests had changed completely and we never could recapture the mutual joys of childhood.

After his illness following George's death, Father never fully recovered his former strength or vitality and began to find the long distances involved by his pastoral visits too much to cover on foot. The whole parish accordingly began secretly to raise money and in this way were able at length to present him with a pony and cart so that he could visit his flock in proper style. For us children, the possession of a horse-drawn vehicle had been beyond our wildest dreams and we were all completely thrilled.

On the other hand it proved to be a mixed blessing because a man had to be employed to drive the gig and look after the pony. This was an added expense that could be ill afforded. For a start there was the cost of feeding the animal and then a new hayloft, stable and shed for the cart had all to be built at the back of the church. The Kirk Session did help out, however, by providing some funds "for pastoral visitation" out of the church offerings. It was our horseman, Jacob, who proved to be the greatest problem though, as he turned out to be a shiftless character and it was impossible to get rid of him since his reputation for idleness was only too well-known and no one else would hire him. Jacob was expected to do all the odd jobs and work in the garden when not driving Father about the parish or attending to the pony and cart but he did little useful work and even his attempts at weeding the flowerbeds or pruning the trees were generally disastrous.

Father now proposed to make regular parish visits two days each week, and on the Sunday before he would announce from the pulpit where he meant to go. He also organised local Bible Hours for the farm workers of the more distant parts of the parish. We were never taken on such ministerial visits but occasionally the whole family would be specially invited out for "tea and scones" – a delight as we grew older, not just on account of the food but because it meant venturing into parts of the parish quite unknown to us before then. We would be most hospitably received in some tiny farm house, generally a two-roomed but-and-ben having the kitchen to one side with its sweet-smelling open peat fire and cooking pot hanging from an iron chain or "swey". To the other side of the front door would be the parlour, never used except for very important visitors like the minister. Everyone lived in the kitchen, sleeping in box beds set either into the walls of the kitchen or in the "treviss" – the short passageway from kitchen to parlour.

I remember a visit we paid to one of Mother's maids, who had married a blacksmith and now lived with her large brood of children in a modest but-and-ben exactly of that kind. She had been grateful to us on account of the gifts Mother used to send for the children and in return gave us all a plain but most welcome afternoon tea. Another visit we all made was to a more distant farm cottage, right at the other side of Cairn William. Our hosts there produced a beautifully made toy horse and cart for Bertie to play with which he absolutely refused to part with when it came time for us to leave. Fortunately the couple assured us that they had no use for it and that Bertie was to keep it.

In the end, our own real pony and cart became worn out and were sold off. Mother in particular was only too glad to see the back of old Jacob who had for too long been a thorn in her flesh.

Will's postponed visit to Germany finally took place in the summer of 1867 and was to prove the first of many. His letters home showed him to be in the highest of spirits and relishing his participation in the distinctive German student clubs of the time. More importantly, he even persuaded Father to come across to the Continent and be his companion on a sight-seeing tour of Germany and Belgium. You can imagine how Father agonised over the proposal and discussed the matter at enormous length with Mother, who insisted she would manage perfectly well in his absence. And at length, after a locum preacher had been found to take his Sabbath place in the pulpit, Father set out, well equipped with warm clothes and an extraordinary variety of pills and potions against the threat of all kinds of illness.

Father and son took great pleasure in this successful joint adventure, their first experience of being together without having the responsibility of looking after the other members of the family. Their journey was crowned by a visit to the Crystal Palace on their return to London and Father came home feeling greatly restored in body and mind, not least from discovering how highly his son was regarded by all his eminent friends and teachers in Germany.

PLEASURES, PASTIMES AND PETS

Now and then we would all take a seaside holiday for several weeks when our parents felt it would be healthy for us to have "a change of air". Sometimes we would go south to Stonehaven, sometimes north to Lossiemouth or Branderburgh on the Moray coast near Elgin. One particular holiday was a nightmare. The house we had rented turned out to be dirty, smelly and far too small for us all. Bertie took ill suddenly and we had to move him into the attic so that he could breathe less tainted air there. Even our drinking water was foul and we could barely find fresh milk, while for some reason the attitude of the local doctor seemed close to being hostile. Mother hardly took a step outside the door and we came back home as soon as Bertie was well enough to travel.

Apart from that one misfortune, all our other seaside holidays were on the whole enjoyable. Every morning we trooped down to the beach for our daily bathe in the sea, provided the weather was fine and the temperature warm enough. First though came the daily ritual of being solemnly "ducked". That was a perfectly horrible experience for me and I could never begin to relax until the ordeal was over. The family rule was that our heads had to be immersed three times at each bathe so that we would become thoroughly accustomed to the experience. Every day without fail therefore the younger children were led out into the sea till we stood waist-high in the water; someone would grasp us firmly by both hands and then, just as a big wave was about to break, our heads would be violently shoved under the surface. Every time it happened I screamed with sheer terror but that only made matters worse because the salt water would choke my mouth and throat until I thought I was drowning.

Yet there was no way out of the dreaded ceremony: our parents were firmly convinced of its curative efficacy. A further drawback for us girls was that our long hair became matted and salty after this immersion and it took ages to comb it out again. But Mother would console us somewhat with one or two cabin biscuits. Then we would be allowed to go bare-footed over the dunes, though the sharp marram grass cut into our tender soles, and then we could paddle freely in the shallows. The boys of course loved sea bathing and were actively encouraged to swim while we girls, for some obscure reason, were definitely not!

On the other hand, we had great fun in and around the beach – although I do recall one dangerous incident in the early days. Our nursemaid set us all to clamber to the top of a big sand dune. My little legs could hardly make the ascent and when I finally reached the top my feet slithered in the soft sand and I came tumbling all the way down, ending up being so completely buried that I thought I was suffocating. Luckily I was pulled out unharmed but Mother was very cross with our nurse and that put an end to such escapades.

Once we met up with another family well known to both my parents. Their boys were not too old to play with us and we discovered from them all the small pleasures of the shore – letting the warm, fine sand run through our fingers or building dams with damp sand from the sea's edge and then waiting eagerly for the tide to break slowly through the barrier, first in a trickle, then in a devastating flood. They showed us too where the nicest shells were to be found – mussels, buckies, cowries and razor-shells – that we later carried home to Keig for decorating our craft work. And the boys even showed us where crabs, sea urchins and sea anemones lurked in the deeper rock pools.

The last summer holiday that we took by the sea must have been in 1871, when I was thirteen. Will was away in Germany again and I was excused from the daily bathing ritual because of a persistent cough that had been bothering me for weeks, especially at nights. It stopped me sleeping, kept the others awake and refused to yield to the usual cough mixture. Before we went on holiday, the doctor was asked if it would be safe for me to go into the water.

"Na, na, Mistress Smith," he said, in his usual blunt fashion. "Keep the young lass oot o the watter. But the sea air'll dae her the warld o guid."

In fact, neither the change of air nor the usual family remedies seemed to make the slightest difference this time. I coughed even more, in spite of sucking cough sweets all day long, and had to sleep in our parents' bedroom to give the others some peace. On the other hand, I was a good deal better during the daytime and my days on the beach were wonderful without the daily threat of total immersion. So I spent the whole of each morning wandering by myself, collecting shellfish and seaweed, splashing in the pools left by the ebbing tide and meticulously searching all the rock pools for starfish, sea anemones, hermit crabs and other small creatures to put into an aquarium that Charlie had made for me. Day after day I trudged home carrying my precious specimens and installed them carefully in the glass case. But for all my trouble none of them survived for long.

Charlie, then seventeen, had brought his fishing rod and could be safely trusted to go off alone to catch fish for tea. Best of all were the flounders that he simply caught with his hands ("guddling" we called it) while wading at the sea's edge. Sometimes we would all trek down to the harbour at break of day to see the herring fleet sail into port with the night's catch. Then homewards we would march carrying a "fry" of freshly caught herring which tasted perfectly delicious for breakfast an hour later, accompanied by large, soft and heavenly-tasting rolls, known locally as "wastels".

When we came home again in September my cough was still worrying my parents and they took the opportunity of asking the advice of an eminent Edinburgh doctor friend who happened to be visiting us that autumn. His advice was that I should be give daily doses of cod-liver oil – and whoever has been forced to take that as a child knows what it tastes like! In addition I was to be wrapped in flannel from head to foot, which was a shocking affront to my girlish vanity. There seemed to be no immediate benefit from that treatment but my cough very gradually disappeared as winter came and went.

Two years previously, in 1869, we had also been on holiday at Lossiemouth and paid a visit early in July to Elgin where we admired the fine ruins of the old cathedral and also went to see the little local museum where, as I told you before, Father had turned the wooden spinning top for Lucy on the lathe. We all slightly envied her for that precious possession and I know I felt a little smug when she later lost it. I still have some shame over that because Father had bought a small wooden bowl for me. But it had not been made by him!

That particular excursion, however, gave us children the chance to carry out a momentous scheme that had been germinating in out minds for quite some time and which I think would hardly have been possible otherwise. Our parents had been married on July 16, 1844, and the date of their silver wedding anniversary was fast approaching. As a rule, events of that kind were not celebrated at all within the family but we were determined that this very special occasion should not go unnoticed and much time was therefore spent discussing how we could possibly organise such an important and delicate matter. Above all it had to be a complete surprise to both parents and therein lay the real difficulty. Will, in Göttingen for the summer, had offered to buy a piece of jewellery on our behalf and send it over but we wanted for once to be entirely independent of our big brother. Moreover, we had decided that the present was to be something useful as well as commemorative. Yet even when we put all our pocket money together, the total amount we could raise – about £3 I think – seemed hopelessly small.

After hours of earnest debate, we made up our minds to buy a new work basket for Mother. This was something she used almost every single day and the old one, which always sat next to her chair, was by now rapidly falling apart. Father, we agreed, ought to have a silver wedding present too and we thought there might be just enough money left over to buy him a fashionable pen of the kind he'd often longed for but had regarded as an unnecessary luxury. Being little more than a village, however, Lossiemouth offered no opportunity to buy either of those gifts. First we thought of taking the train into Aberdeen but that was a hopeless idea on two counts: we hadn't money to waste on train fares and we knew also that it would be impossible to find an excuse to go without telling our parents an outright lie, which was of course quite unthinkable. So the trip to Elgin came just in time.

Having put our heads together again, we came up with an elaborate plan of campaign. It was agreed that, once we all been to see the cathedral and museum, Nellie and Charles should quietly disappear in search of shops likely to have what we wanted. If either Father or Mother asked where they were, the rest of us were to say they had just gone off together to explore the town. That didn't seem too desperate a falsehood.

About an hour later the pair arrived back looking quietly

pleased with themselves and, one after another, we all found a chance to ask them in whispers how they had fared. I managed to sidle up to Nellie.

"Well, have you managed it?" I asked breathlessly.

"Everything's taken care of. We've got both presents. Inside our budget too!"

"Where have you hidden them?" This had been our constant worry – how to get the presents home, especially the basket, without the parents finding out.

"That's all taken care of too. Charles has the pen but the shop is going to deliver the basket to the station. We'll pick it up from there."

Though Nellie sounded perfectly confident, I was much less convinced that we could travel all the way home without such a bulky parcel being noticed by either parent. But it all turned out much more straightforward than I had feared. Coming back from such a lengthy holiday, we had a great mass of luggage to deal with and Father was kept busy seeing that all the trunks and bags were safely stowed in the luggage van.

Charles meantime fussed around Mother, pretending to make sure she was comfortably installed in the carriage beside Bertie, Lucy and me, and then he announced, "It's far too cramped in here for all of us. Nellie and I will find ourselves another compartment. That'll give everybody much more room."

It all sounded very plausible and no questions were asked. The work basket was safely smuggled on board and the train set off. More problems loomed ahead though. When our train reached the junction at Kintore, the stationmaster yelled out, "Change here for Alford! All change for Alford!" I had completely forgotten about that difficulty but Charles and Nellie had not. In all the fluster of moving our luggage on to the branch line train, neither parent noticed one bulky extra parcel. The final hurdle was at Whitehouse Station where we all got off. Charlie and Nellie again rose to the occasion and somehow contrived to arrange with the stationmaster that he should keep the parcel secretly until they could collect it the following day.

By this time of course we were all, apart from Charlie, in a high state of excitement, a state of affairs which should have alerted Mother at least to the fact that something strange was going on. In any case, our exaggerated nonchalance, our singing and our barging about on the platform ought to have aroused some suspicions. Homecomings after being on holiday were never quite so cheerful as that. Our successful intrigue had, we concluded, been a miracle of cunning and strategy.

Or had it? In retrospect, I think our parents must have long since found out what was happening. But certainly the surprise and joy shown by both parents seemed utterly genuine to us all next morning when they came into the kitchen and found both gifts on the breakfast table.

* * * *

Coming home after several weeks at the seaside always had ample compensations. I would rush straightaway into the garden to see how everything was growing and especially to discover if the gooseberries were ripe. That year the bushes were simply laden with juicy fruit. Our maid, who had not been with us that year, reported that Nellie's Calla lily, which had never bloomed before, was now in flower. Well, that was something of an exaggeration but it had at least sprouted a very long, elegantly curved shaft and was beginning to open out. There were weeds everywhere however and when we walked to the gate leading to the church (the one we called the Church Walk) the usually trim borders where the blackcurrant bushes grew were thick with two foot high groundsel. I couldn't wait to get at the stuff and first thing next day was outside, determined to tackle the weeds on my own, only to find that Father had been there before me and had cleared one patch. At fifty-eight he still enjoyed working in his garden and, as I have mentioned, his efforts to find a man capable of doing some of the heavier tasks properly were usually fruitless. No one we employed ever showed the slightest feeling for gardening and Mother would throw up her hands in despair when she invariably found the hired man pulling out all her carefully tended seedlings along with the weeds. Only as a last resort therefore would she allow any such "helpers" near the flowerbeds.

Even more than my sisters, I was keen to help as much as possible in the garden; but lessons always had to come first, followed by our various duties in the house. So my gardening hours had to be snatched from whatever free time was left at the end of the day or before breakfast. Maybe I did prove more of a help to Father than the others but even so I was very much taken by surprise when one day he handed me money, saying, "Alice, away you go into Alford and buy yourself a straw boater."

I was overjoyed at the wholly unexpected and quite uncharacteristic gesture but duly came home proudly wearing my smart new garden bonnet, which I decorated with a band of bright blue cotton around the brim. On another occasion he presented me with a brand new spade, lighter and smaller than the one he used himself, which made the labour of digging much easier. Gifts of this kind were very rare events indeed and those instances were probably Father's roundabout way of expressing his gratitude for the work I had done. He would never have actually expressed such feelings in words.

77

One summer Nellie and I made plans to clear the big shrubbery at the front of the house. The soil there had lain undisturbed for years and was infested with ground elder (we Presbyterians called it bishop-weed) whose long white roots rampaged through the earth. If the least bit of the roots was left behind, next year would find the ground as thickly covered as ever with the dreaded infestation. So every spadeful of earth had to be carefully sifted through by hand to eradicate all trace of the rootlets. Though we started out on this project by ourselves, Mother and Father soon saw what we were up to and expressed their disapproval. "It's far too much for you both," said Mother.

"Aye, and you'll never see the end of it," added Father pessimistically.

Sadly, he was entirely right. As usual we started off with great verve and eventually managed to clear a substantial area of bishop-weed but our enthusiasm waned as we gradually came to realise it was a losing battle. Nellie gave up first, claiming other demands on her time. Then I decided to tackle another weed-infested spot on my own – one of the gooseberry beds – but ended up so badly scratched by the thorns from the bushes that I finally gave up in despair.

By now it was becoming plain that the whole garden was really too much for Father and his dwindling band of maiden helpers. In any case, both Nellie and I were due to go off with Will to Edinburgh that autumn of 1869. So we decided to turn all our attention to the flowerbeds and were able at least to keep those at the front looking presentable. At the back of the house, where the ground sloped upwards more steeply, Father's fine garden slowly but surely became a wilderness. Father ironically called it "the wilderness of Sin".

For a few years after that, we did have the services of a very deaf old man, though we couldn't afford to employ him on a regular basis and he mainly helped to plant and harvest the potatoes and vegetables. I can't really say he was a good worker, since he enjoyed nothing better than to lean on his spade and engage any of us in lengthy chats. I avoided him especially because he could never make out what I was saying in my rather small voice. On the other hand, he seemed well enough able to understand Lucy and she for her part seemed only too happy to gossip for ages with the poor fellow.

Gardening was normally a voluntary task but there were exceptions. In early summer, lessons stopped at noon sharp and we were all press-ganged into weeding the vegetables beds before the seedlings became suffocated. Even Mother joined in and each of us had a board to squat on, together with a big enamel basin for the weeds. The beds were narrow enough for us to reach right across without stepping on the earth at all. At least, that was the theory! Father approached the whole business with great seriousness, as if it were a military operation, and a sharp rebuke came to any child who trod on a plant, missed a weed or broke the stalk off so that the roots remained in the earth. My back used to get quite sore even at that age and I sighed with relief when we had finished for the day.

Then there was the berry-picking in late summer – mainly our gooseberries and blackcurrants. We did have raspberries but the blackbirds seemed to get to most of these first. For this job we would all muster immediately after breakfast, each with a jug from which we slowly filled the big wicker laundry basket with the day's harvest. Then Mother would make jam in large quantities to send off to our friends in the city. Berry-picking lasted the whole morning without a break and if there was still more ripe fruit we were set to the task again in the afternoon. For all that, it was pleasant enough, working away, chatting together in the fresh air and helping ourselves now and then to the choicest berries.

Father had a firm if over-optimistic belief in the medical efficacy of various pills and, being something of a hypochondriac, swallowed an incredible quantity of these. Naturally he believed in similarly dosing all his children with pills whenever they took ill – as happened only too frequently. None of us found it easy to swallow pills in a single gulp without water, so we would practice the art out in the garden using blackcurrants. The others managed this quite easily but I invariably ended up with the berry still in my mouth, to the great amusement of the others but to my own embarrassment.

One year Lucy and I decided to establish a flowerbed of our own in an uncultivated bit of woodland adjoining the main garden and just next to the little workshop that Charles and the other boys had built for their own use. Though small, we planned it out beforehand, with carefully designed pathways and parterres, imagining that we were playing the part of Mother's uncle, James Giles, who (you'll remember) had helped the Marquis of Aberdeen to plan out the great parkland at Haddo House. Our plants were all taken as seedlings from the wooded slopes beyond the garden and were therefore not especially elegant. Never mind; this was our own secret creation and kept up happily occupied over those summer months, until one day disaster struck! We woke up to discover that some cows had strayed in and flattened our precious piece of land to a muddy wasteland. We were furious and complained bitterly to the herd lad responsible.

"It must never, never happen again, do you understand?" we said severely. "Just you keep these beasts of yours under control."

But the uncouth herd loon just laughed in our faces. That time we were able to remake our private garden reasonably well but by the autumn the cows got in again and this time destroyed it completely. That was the end of our collective enterprise but I still had my own small patch which had been sadly neglected all the while.

We four sisters, Bella, Nellie, Lucy and I, had lots of other recreations in the early days. Once, when our parents were away, we decided to hold a tea party for our brothers and carefully wrote out invitations in our best handwriting:

The Misses Smith, of 2 The Nursery Square, Keig,
request the attendance of Master Bertie Smith
at a tea party to be held this Friday at three o'clock
within 1 Parlour Terrace, Keig

R.S.V.P.

And then we carefully penned the same for Will, George and Charlie. The tea party fare was of the simplest – home-made biscuits or oat-cakes and butter – washed down with a fruit drink that we concocted ourselves. But that had been when I was much younger. Now only Lucy and I were still at the stage of playing pretend games of this kind and one day the pair of us decided to host a special dinner party for the grown-ups. The main course was to be a dumpling made with oatmeal that we would have harvested and ground all by ourselves – a business which turned out so long and difficult that I quickly regretted the whole idea.

We were always free to glean corn at harvest time for our rabbits' food store; even so, gathering a sheaf large enough for grinding into a bowlful of oatmeal took us days. Then we had to thresh it with a home-made flail, winnow the chaff and husk the grain. That in particular was an interminable business and tried my patience sorely. Finally, grinding the corn with a large stone was relatively easy and satisfying.

Now, we thought, it was safe to fix a time and date for the dinner party. As our parents were at home, "Parlour Terrace" was unavailable and we arranged that the entertainment should take place out of doors in a suitably sheltered bower at one end of the garden, the dumpling to arrive ceremoniously on a wooden platter which I had carved myself.

Suet for the dumpling was beyond our resources and had to be begged from the kitchen. Neither of us, however, had any idea about the proper quantity of fat to use and by the time we had proudly carried the dumpling to the waiting guests it had more or less disintegrated. Though it certainly tasted a bit odd, we were assured by all that it was a truly excellent dumpling.

"Oh, a very fine dumpling indeed," remarked Father, parodying Dr Johnson. But I didn't rate it one of our successes.

When our own powers of imagination wore out, we always turned to Will for ideas. During the University vacations, and especially if the weather was bad, we could always rely on him to come up with a new game.

"Ahoy, you children aloft!" he'd shout to us. "At five o'clock I'll climb the rigging for a game with you. Be ready and waiting."

And with the striking of the big manse clock, he would arrive in the nursery to play Blind Man's Buff until the normally tranquil house was echoing with the noise of footsteps and laughter. On summer evenings he would try to set aside an hour for us before dinner to play some special game outside with intricate rules of his own devising.

On free evenings he would take us for walks – he went so fast that I always got a stitch in my side – and, just as Father had done when Will himself was a boy, would provide us with a running commentary on all the wonders of nature –

the different cloud formations and their names; the reason for the blue colour of the sky ("according to Professor Tyndall anyway," Will said); the ways in which heat was conveyed by radiation, convection or conduction; and the geological formations on neighbouring Bennachie. It was a special thrill for me to be allowed to climb all the way to the top of Cairn William with Will, even though it was so tiring to struggle through the deep heather. From the top, as I told you earlier, we had a magnificent view of the mountains beyond us to the west and of the sea to the north and east. That was the time we caught the baby hare among the heather. Events like those brought us all home exhausted but invigorated and radiant.

Winter kept us indoors a great deal, all the more so because our parents had grown increasingly anxious over health matters since the deaths of Mary Jane and George. As a special privilege we were now allowed to join the grown-ups in the sitting-room, which, along with the nursery, was of course the only heated room in the house other than the kitchen. The noise of our chatter was distracting though, especially to Father, and Will would often offer to give us each a penny if we could stay perfectly quiet for a quarter of an hour. That was very hard even with the promise of a reward and it was more fun to try to make one of the others lose. So we would quietly make ugly faces at one another until somebody exploded with laughter. Life became very dull indeed whenever Will had to leave us at the end of the holidays.

As we grew older, Will invented a highly appropriate game for our Sunday evenings. We children all sat down at the big table, each with our own Bible open in front of us. He would then walk up and down while we took turns to choose an obscure verse from the Bible, one which had no obvious clue to the context and which

therefore was as difficult as possible. The challenge of
course was for Will to identify the exact source of the
quotation – book, chapter and verse. So complete was his
memory of the whole Bible that we could hardly ever catch
him out and he would usually give us chapter and verse
without hesitation, adding for good measure the Hebrew of
the Old Testament verses preceding the one we had selected.
Only once did I manage to find a verse from one of the
Minor Prophets which completely stumped him. On another
occasion I tried him out with the same verse and again
caught him out.

"It's no good, Alice. For some reason that verse won't
stick in my mind." Unfortunately I now can't recall it
myself!

When Will was away we still managed to amuse ourselves
fairly well with the help of Charlie and the boarders. On the
playground ("Grissand") we enjoyed *Kivi*, a version of *Qui
vive*, and another, similar but on a bigger scale, that we
called *Guard the Treasure, Charlie*, played in the field
adjoining the church. For the latter we were in two opposing
teams, each with a leader. The aim was to steal the other
side's treasure (a pile of sticks) by means of a bold run into
their territory. If caught, however, an opponent was put into
"prison" until released by someone from the own side. This
was a thrilling game for us and could go on for a long time
before either side gained total control.

Each of us, as you know, had our own pair of stilts and
through long practice became quite skilled in walking and
even running on these. Naturally we invented stilt games,
involving a narrow, twisting course that had to be negotiated
without falling off. That could be made harder still by
having to avoid touching one another. Every so often bows
and arrows came briefly into season and then the manse roof
would be festooned with arrows after we had held a

wappenshaw to see who could fire their arrows right over the house.

In autumn, skipping became the girls' favourite sport, especially as that activity was guaranteed to keep us warm. The real skipping ropes Nellie brought Lucy and me from Germany with proper hand grips were a decided improvement on the miscellaneous lengths of old clothes-rope we were accustomed to use before then. Now we were able to skip all the way down the road for Mother's messages, as long as the ground was dry enough. The road to Whitehouse was usually deserted except for the occasional farm cart. Every so often, however, there would be tree-felling on the estate and then we had to walk gingerly along the tops of the stone dykes to avoid the enormous loads of timber being dragged on trailers by big teams of horses.

The croquet set our ever-thoughtful eldest brother had sent us gave constant pleasure. Charlie, being the carpentry expert, had made a fine rack out of birch wood to hold the mallets, hoops and balls. There was no decent lawn at the house so again we used the park or grassy field beside the church. This sloped more steeply than was ideal for a croquet lawn, but that made the game all the more testing, though the small playing area compensated for that. Knowing all the bumps and ridges on the surface, we always had an advantage over our visitors who were invariably pressed into playing croquet, sometimes much against their inclination.

Our old bachelor friend (with the cherry tree) became passionately fond of the game but had no scruples about cheating and grew quite furious if he was beaten. Some of the parishioners, invited for afternoon tea, were less enthusiastic but were far too polite to demur and later could at least boast of having "played croquet with the Doctor himsel". Actually Father mostly felt it more dignified to act as referee and coach but frequently got so carried away that he would abruptly grab hold of a player's mallet and try to show just how it *should* be done! In that respect, Will and Father were temperamentally very much alike – neither suffered fools gladly. As you know, when we played chess, Father behaved in just the same fashion, having some lingering scruples about the propriety of playing a secular game of that kind, yet always looking over our shoulders and whispering advice, being absolutely convinced that he alone knew the finer points of strategy. He never knew how frustrated we became when he interfered because none of us dared show our irritation.

The household routine required, quite properly, that no one should ever be late for meals. For us children this was as rigorous as any law of the Medes and Persians, yet we found it difficult to be on time when wandering far out of doors since none of us had a watch. Father therefore opted quite successfully for the Australian method of cupping his hands round his mouth and calling out "Co-ee! Co-ee!" a few minutes before dinner. It was a surprisingly clear and penetrating sound, albeit not entirely in keeping with his ministerial status, and whenever we heard the call we came running helter-skelter homewards.

Inflexible as the household rule of mealtime punctuality was intended to be, an exception was made in the case of croquet. This was usually played during the short period of free time before dinner and all too often a game had just reached its most critical and exciting point when dinner was announced. If we children alone had been playing there would have been no latitude whatsoever in the matter; however, with one or both parents as closely involved spectators, a dispensation was given. "Well, bairns, you can play ten minutes more but no longer!"

In a ministerial family, playing at cards was of course strictly ruled out. Well, almost. One long, severe winter, Will arrived home from Edinburgh bearing a pack of cards and explained in a very matter-of-fact manner that he thought it would be a good idea to teach us youngsters whist. Then we could have something to do if the weather stayed bad. We were quite stunned by this, knowing Father's attitude on the subject of such a devilish practice; but Will had a long talk with both parents, explaining that the game would be quite a harmless distraction for us in the bad weather – and would keep us all quietly occupied. The outcome confirmed what I had long suspected, that Will nowadays could invariably get his way simply because Father and Mother now had such complete faith in his judgement.

The only qualification was that we should *never, never* play for money. So in these dark wintry afternoons, after lessons, Will taught us whist, a game he had learned to play in Edinburgh with Professor Tait and his wife. To my great surprise, Mother also took part eagerly, and that provided a pleasant alternative occupation for her otherwise restless hands. Father of course professed to have no time to waste on such dangerous frivolities.

Over the years we had a great variety and quantity of pets. These were a special childhood pleasure, not least because their births and deaths allowed us to commemorate those events with suitably solemn childhood rituals. Beside our own woodland garden, for example, stood the graves of two white rabbits which had been fatally mauled by the family cat after it had squeezed through a small hole in the netting of their hutch. We held an imposing funeral to mark the sad occasion and then erected a headstone of slate, surrounded by wattle fencing that we had painstakingly woven out of willow. On the slate we engraved their joint epitaph:

Here lie our two white rabbits dear
No more the cat's cruel claws they'll fear;
Like flowers with scarcely opened blooms
Our rabbits rest within their tombs.

Sadly, the rabbits' resting-place suffered the same fate as the woodland garden and was trampled underfoot by straying cows. Over the years, however, we kept scores of tame rabbits, sometimes a dozen or more at any one time. This gave us a lot of work and simply finding enough food for them was a major problem in itself. All the kitchen leftovers went to feed our pig and the two cows we kept for milk.

The parental rule in this case was: *Keep as many rabbits as you like but find the food for them yourselves!* Every time we went out for a walk, therefore, we had to search for suitable rabbit food in the fields and hedgerows, carrying it carefully home in our pinafores if we had no other container handy. Dandelions were always appreciated by the rabbits and were usually plentiful enough, except in winter; so also were sow-thistle and clover. But we could never build up a proper reserve of food and so the foraging had to be done on a daily basis – complicated by the fact that Sunday walks were not allowed. As Nellie observed, we were just like the Israelites in the wilderness, forced to gather double quantities of manna on the day before each Sabbath if our rabbits were to survive till Monday.

Whenever we contrived to visit our friend the old bachelor with the cherry tree, we would offer to do some tidying up for him and would then be certain of getting a whole load of juicy weeds – enough to last for three days anyway. His garden was full of willow herb by August and our pets liked it so much that we used to call it "rabbit-herb". At home, in the field opposite the manse, we were occasionally allowed to gather some of the hay. The owner happened to be a brother of our bachelor friend but was much more irascible and so we had to be extremely diplomatic in our dealings with him, especially as both parents had warned us to stay off his ground in wet weather. If stocks of foods ran really low, one of us would have to creep out stealthily after dark to get supplies.

In winter time it became impossible to find food for all our rabbits, so Mother would buy them from us for one shilling and sixpence apiece, sometimes even more if it was a particularly fine fat specimen. Pocket money always had to be *earned* in some way or another and I suspect that our being encouraged to keep so many pet rabbits was in fact a rather clever parental strategy for supplementing the manse larder. During autumn we went gleaning in the newly harvested fields, like Ruth in the Bible, to collect a store of straw for the rabbits' bedding. If the corn sheaves still stood in their neat stooks, we felt morally justified in helping ourselves to a small bundle from a sheaf or two, on the principle laid down by Robert Burns – that "a daimen icker in a thrave's a sma' request" and would not be missed.

The turnip harvest was much more profitable though. We would line the road as the cartloads passed and then run after any stray turnips that fell off – unless of course the driver took the trouble to chase us off and pick them up himself. One farmer was particularly benevolent and would always turn a blind eye to our scavenging. Even with those rich pickings though, the rabbit's food store was never enough to see them right through the winter and our pets inevitably became sacrifices for the dinner table.

We kept pet pigeons in much the same way as the rabbits until they proved too much of a nuisance by pecking off all the garden peas. Some friends once gave Lucy and me a

89

baby pigeon which had fallen out of its nest. We called it Iris and for a time it became our own special pet, so tame it would come to our hands as soon as we went to the back door and called out, "Iris, Iris!" Nellie composed a song for it:

Come down to me, O Iris dear;
Our work is done and we are here.

And a good deal more of the same doggerel. One day Iris suddenly disappeared and we feared the worst. A couple of days later she turned up again but had lost all her attachment to humans.

We tried hand-rearing young red squirrels also, feeding them on nuts, seeds and fruit, but they always managed to escape back to the wild. Hedgehogs we fed on milk, bread and berries but they too generally disappeared, though one became quite domesticated and used to run, pit-a-pat, pit-a-pat, up and down the long lobby that led from the front door to the kitchen. The boys once tried rearing baby owls too and were reasonably successful for a time. They housed the owlets in a box by the Grissand playground where the mother owl came regularly by night to feed them until they were fully-fledged and quietly flew away.

Naturally there was always our household cat too, born on the very same day in 1862 as Bertie, while Nellie had her own canary that sang most sweetly, though Mother complained it always gave her a headache since it used to join in whenever she began using her sewing machine. So the canary had to be silenced then by having a blanket thrown over its cage. The most exotic of our pets was, I think, a turtle that our parents once brought from Aberdeen, no doubt simply because neither we nor they had ever seen a live turtle before. But it survived only briefly, even though we added handfuls of salt to the water in a despairing effort to provide it with the equivalent of briny seawater.

Our parents seemed to approve of all our efforts with the pets but kept a sharp eye on their welfare. Every evening, as long as the weather was fine, it was their regular custom to stroll arm in arm around the garden, admiring the plants, pointing out the birds' nests in the trees and inspecting whatever animals we were keeping in residence at the time. The manse cat, however, was the chief danger for our little Noah's Ark and it was impossible for us to keep a constant eye on her marauding excursions.

One morning we were learning Geography, Mother having decided to delegate to Bella the duty of instructing Lucy and me in the subject. The lessons took a curious form since our elder sister loathed the role of teacher and displayed her lack of enthusiasm openly, while we in turn were rapidly bored by a task that required no more than rote memory for the small number of geographical facts that Bella herself had acquired. A large map of the world hung on the nursery wall and Bella stood rather limply beside it, calling out the name of a country, river, sea or city to each of us in turn. We then grabbed the long pointer and raced to locate whichever spot she had named.

"Lucy, find the . . . Zambesi River!"

"Alice, show me . . . er, the Himalayas!"

And so on. Since we very soon got to know every single feature on the map, the only real interest lay in seeing how quickly we could do the game. Suddenly the door opened and Bertie rushed in breathlessly.

"C-c-c-cat's got b-b-b-blackie's nest," he stammered in high excitement. Sure enough, when we got there, the nest was lying on the ground, empty of its nestlings. So we set off to find the cat, breathing the most dreadful threats.

"Let's get rid of that horrible cat once and for all," said Lucy.

"Kill him, I say. Let's string him up. Let's have a proper hanging," was my shameless proposal.

All that afternoon we hunted, high and low, for the manse cat, determined to exact vengeance for the atrocity we felt she had committed. But the cat was nowhere to be found. Clever animal that she was, I think she sensed both her own wrongdoing and the danger she was now in. That evening, we sat in solemn conclave to decide what to do and confirmed our resolution to make her pay the ultimate penalty. Charlie even offered to tie a stone round its neck and fling it over Telford's high-arched bridge at Keig into the river Don. Next day indeed we found the culprit, who scratched and hissed as it fought for its life, but fate stepped in just as we were about to carry out our dreadful deed. Possibly Mother had somehow got wind of our intentions. Anyway, a visiting neighbour walked out into the garden as the little lynch mob stood holding the condemned animal.

"My, bairns, but that's a grand pussy bawdrons ye've got there. Mebbe ye'd let me tak her hame. She'll rid me o the rats in the stable."

There was of course no choice but to accept this last-minute reprieve. Some of us, I think, felt glad about it. Others among us still believed that justice had not been properly done. Our parents said nothing one way or another either about the cat's actions or our own sentiments. Instead, they sternly expressed their disapproval of our wild and unruly behaviour in abandoning the Geography lesson. As a result the class was quietly dropped from our curriculum. Bella complained bitterly though that our lack of discipline had shown total disrespect for her as the big sister.

For a time our favourite pet was a robin. Although many robins came to the big garden in winter for food, only one robin became tame enough to beg for food by tapping at the window pane until we lifted the sash and spread a handful of oatcake crumbs on the sill. Soon it became trusting enough to hop on to our outstretched palms and peck at the crumbs we held. Then it grew bold enough to tap at our parents' bedroom window and even Mother couldn't resist giving it some breakfast in the same way. With the coming of spring, the robin suddenly disappeared until some weeks later, when Lucy and I were in the woodlands just beyond the garden, a robin fearlessly hopped up to us, demanding to be fed. We were certain this must be our old pet and, sure enough, after some patient searching, we found its nest hidden deep under a hedgerow. And inside, to our amazement, were four small fledglings.

When we told our story that evening over dinner, the whole family wanted to view the nest. We allowed this but only under strict conditions, for fear of scaring the mother robin and her chicks. Only one visitor at a time was permitted and we demanded from everyone a handful of crumbs as admission fee. That system worked so well that the mother bird was in danger of growing completely lazy and forgetting her maternal duties. In those days we had no thoughts about the effects of such meddling.

Last of all, our pet seagull ought to be mentioned. We had brought her back home in a large cardboard box from one of our seaside holidays on the justification that she had a broken wing and therefore needed our careful ministrations. When we released her in the garden, she reacted aggressively and wouldn't tolerate a close approach by humans. Bertie was very scared and even Lucy was uneasy with the seagull, who seemed to sense their fear instinctively. Even the cat met its match with her and suffered by having her tail pecked continually. The odd thing was that if Father went towards her, wagging his finger at her in stern reproach, she immediately crept away. We kept her for quite some time, until she began to wander off and one day returned no more.

OUTWARD BOUND

All the girls in our family had their regular education from Mother: first the elements of reading, writing and arithmetic, then history and geography as we grew older. History started with the Romans, Picts and Scots; then we progressed to the kings and queens of Britain, learning by heart all their names and the length of their various reigns. We were also expected to memorise the names and dates of the European monarchs, but the emphasis was always on British history. Then came some sketchy geography of the kind I've described, followed by elementary grammar lessons. Religious instruction was of course an essential part of each day's teaching – Mother considered handwork and Bible study both to be of equal and prime importance.

From the earliest possible age, as you know, we would go downstairs on Sunday mornings to the living-room where Mother would read Bible stories to us from the Old and New Testaments. Needless to say, the text was that of the Authorised Version and Mother took it for granted that its scriptural word was sufficient: so she seldom if ever considered it necessary to give any additional explanation. Nor did we ourselves think it of the least importance to understand the background or meaning of those stories. As guides to the Bible history, however, we did have coloured cards giving details of all the biblical events from the Creation in 4004 BC onwards to the coming of Christ.

Those Sunday lessons continued week by week as we grew up and everyone in the household was expected to attend, apart from Father who always rested before taking the church service. Over time, the shape of the lessons changed only in the sense of becoming more demanding, until eventually we were expected to prepare in advance two whole chapters from the Old Testament each week – as well as learning our two psalms by heart.

Sunday morning catechism formed an essential part of our religious instruction. Mother posed the questions, one by one, to each of us in turn and if our answer showed any inaccuracy she would prompt us and very occasionally explain the sense more fully. Knowing the Shorter Catechism was felt to be much more than just an intellectual exercise. Mother and Father both emphasised to us that our knowledge of the catechism would be a lifelong bulwark against all the worldly dangers and temptations to which we would be exposed.

Learning all one hundred and fifty questions and answers from the Shorter Catechism was a lengthy, trying business and each of us was expected to practise the task to ourselves every day at any spare moment. For all the tedium of such repetitive learning, I often felt later in life that it had been a valuable experience for us and that I had somehow benefited tangibly from knowing my catechism so thoroughly. So I was grateful for all Mother's efforts. She always insisted that the Shorter Catechism embraced the entire doctrine of Christianity.

What is Man's chief end? was the opening question; and the well-known answer was automatically offered up:

Man's chief end is to glorify God and enjoy Him for ever.

I still firmly believe that the world would be a better place if everyone acknowledged the glorification of God to be the most important rule of life.

Coming near the end of the catechism came the harder question, *What is prayer?* – to which the answer was:

Prayer is the offering up of our desires unto God for things agreeable to His will, with confession of our sins and thankful acknowledgement of His mercies.

For me, that seemed an admirably clear and comprehensive explanation of prayer. Whenever one of us had a birthday, Mother would signal the event by calling us into her bedroom for some solemn words of advice, followed by a brief prayer.

Mother's main aim for our secular education as girls and young women was to have us become capable, useful daughters and wives. Sewing and knitting, along with mending and darning, were obligatory accomplishments and we learned these very thoroughly and systematically under Mother's expert guidance.

A major undertaking for each of us was the sewing of our personal samplers on which all the letters of the alphabet, along with the numerals up to ten, were meticulously embroidered in cross-stitch. Below these were stitched the initials of all the family members: the living in red, the dead in black, in token of the divine principle: *In the midst of Life we are in Death.* Last of all, I was meant to embroider my name in full – Alice Smith – but ran out of space and so had to shorten it to read just *Alice Sm*, followed by the date of completion.

Mother's own sampler, which hung on the nursery wall, was a much grander affair than any of ours: it had complicated decorative patterns as well as little houses and trees. I dearly longed to do something just as elaborate but was firmly told such indulgences were quite unnecessary – the whole purpose of the sampler was to teach us how to form characters and numbers – not to provide us with pleasure.

Lots of sheep belonging to Lord Forbes' estate grazed in

the woodlands above the manse garden and whenever we went for hill walks we would gather the wool that had been caught in the fencing or in the trees themselves. Mother promised that when we had collected enough to fill a large bag she would have it spun into yarn and then she would teach Lucy and me to knit stockings. First though we had to clean all the wool very thoroughly and then tease it out – an awkward and lengthy job for our inexpert hands which all too easily picked up nasty splinters from the wooden fences.

Still, we were very keen to knit stockings for Bertie and so we persevered. Off went the wool to Alford and back it came eventually, beautifully spun into knitting yarn. The pair of us then set to work to knit one stocking apiece under Mother's instruction during the winter afternoons. Unfortunately, Lucy knitted much too loosely while I knitted very tightly so that the two stockings were completely unequal in size. And both turned out anyway to be far too small for Bertie, much to our disappointment. Mother, as usual, came up with the answer. "You can just take the stockings up the road to Margaret. They'll be just grand for her new bairn."

Margaret had been one of our maidservants and seemed delighted with our gift for her baby. "Ye're twa richt braw knitters, I maun say," she said. "Come awa ben the hoose for a cuppie tea and play wi the wee laddie. Hae a blether wi George as weel. He's fair weariet nae being fit tae wark."

A forestry worker on the estate, her husband George had injured his knee very badly and had been unable to do any work for months. That meant great hardship for the family yet somehow they survived, thanks to the support of friends and neighbours. George was certainly pleased enough to see "the bairns frae the Manse" and insisted on showing off his damaged leg which we duly viewed, half in curiosity and half in horror, the whole of his knee joint having turned a rich brown colour from the over-liberal application of iodine, which only recently had become the favoured treatment for flesh wounds. That put both of us off making a return visit for many months.

* * * *

When we were judged old enough, Lucy and I were allowed to do some of our own lessons in Father's study, where he now taught Charlie and the boarders, joined later by Bertie. By then, of course, Will and George were at Aberdeen University. Father's educational ideals were different from Mother's and for any of us girls to graduate to this privileged level we had to show sufficient intellectual ability and also demonstrate a sincere dedication to learning. Mostly I was happy to work hard under his instruction but there were certainly some difficult moments.

In a way, Father had been spoiled by the sheer brilliance of his two eldest sons and found it frustrating to have to accept lower standards from any of us. So his fussiness, irritability and sheer impatience showed itself increasingly. Poor Bertie, who was by far the slowest of all his children, suffered most of all. Father seemed incapable of grasping that Latin was beyond his youngest child and so couldn't hide his exasperation at Bertie's unavailing attempts to conjugate *amo, amas, amat.* A classical education, in Father's eyes, was the only effective foundation for any young man aspiring to professional status in later life and a firm grasp of Latin was the key to all future success. So Bertie suffered constantly from Father's wrath while Lucy and I felt agonies of pity for our little brother.

Worst of all was the hour of study immediately after tea and evening worship. By then Father's patience was at its most brittle and we girls would desperately try to finish our work so that we could escape from the inevitable crisis when, in a frenzy of impotent rage, Father would fling the textbook at Bertie's head and shout in broad Scots, "Awa, ye great sumph! Awa till yer bed."

Being eager to learn, I was lucky because my enthusiasm and diligence pleased Father. The others often taunted me though with being his pet and compared me invidiously to Jacob's favourite son, Joseph. I'm certain that neither of our parents ever *consciously* favoured one of their children above the others – their high standards of justice prevented that – but undoubtedly they did value the brightest of their offspring more than the others. Will's achievements at Aberdeen, Edinburgh and beyond, for example, set goals that most of us could never realistically aspire to and we all knew, without envy, that Will was indeed the apple of Father's eye.

Even for me, learning did not always go smoothly. Father began to teach me Latin at an early age but suddenly abandoned the effort. Probably I was finding it far too difficult. Nevertheless, no explanation was given and I felt quite humiliated at this snub. Then he decided I should learn some French with him but that also proved a dismal failure. There was no proper textbook available in the manse, only some ancient primer. I can't recall how old I was when this began but I became convinced that Father himself didn't fully understand the principles of French grammar, even though he could read French tolerably well.

Matters came to a head one day when he and I disagreed over a particular French idiom, and the lessons were forthwith halted, much to my distress at what seemed a second rejection. In secret I wept bitterly because I so much wanted to be as successful as Will or George. Curiously enough, Charlie too had suffered from his father's ire through being a poor classical scholar, though brilliant at Maths.

By the age of eleven, I was growing increasingly restless. Will was by then well-established in Edinburgh, studying theology at New College, and Nellie, seven years older than I was and already a confident young woman, had accompanied him there as housekeeper and was allowed to attend an Edinburgh school, much to my intense envy. When she came home during the vacations, she began to teach me French again and gave both Lucy and me piano lessons.

I was delighted with this chance of acquiring a new accomplishment but found it hard to find the time to practise amongst all the other daily demands on my time. Lucy and I would take turn about to get up early and put in an hour's practice before breakfast. Often though it was barely light and by autumn the morning chill of the unheated parlour meant that our fingers soon became stiff with the cold. At the best of times our hands suffered badly from the winter cold and Mother, who put the blame on the slates that we used for our arithmetic, knitted mittens for us all. I tried wearing these for piano practice but even that proved no answer.

By this time I was turning into a distinctly nervy, anxious child. I began to suffer various aches and pains in my bones, which I put down to the ice-cold piano practice sessions, but which some today would probably attribute to emotional problems. One Sunday I had seen a man having an epileptic fit in church and that experience tortured me for months. At my morning piano practice, I would sit in a torment of anxiety, looking fearfully over my shoulder in case the man was lurking behind me. Those irrational fears and physical pains were to recur over the years. I personally believe they were physical rather than psychological in origin and signalled the beginning of the back problems that were to last for most of my life.

At long last came the most important event of my whole childhood. It was September, 1869, and I was eleven and a half years old. After spending two months in Germany, at Heidelberg and Göttingen, Will by now had been captivated by Germany partly because of its pre-eminence at that time in both mathematics and science but still more so for its advanced theological ideas. We had no idea then of the problems that were later to arise between him and the Free Church because of these influences. Will was back with us by the end of August and was due to return to Edinburgh in late October for his final year at New College. As usual I was beginning to dread his departure because whenever he was away life at the manse seemed to lose all sparkle and grow drearily dull.

Then one day, quite out of the blue, he pulled me aside and asked, "Alice, how would you like to come to Edinburgh with Nellie and me? Maybe you could even go to school there."

I almost leapt into the air with delight at the proposal. "Oh, Will, that would be just wonderful!" Then doubts immediately began to assail me.

"Do you think *they* would allow it?" There was no need to specify who "they" were.

"We'll have to ask them both, that's all," said Will. "It must be their decision, you know that."

My eldest brother would never have said otherwise. But I now knew how well he could handle both parents and how completely trusting they had become of his judgement. Even so, several days of obvious tension followed at home before Father and Mother finally agreed they could allow me to do as Will had suggested.

He imposed his own condition though. "Before I take you to Edinburgh, Alice, you simply must get rid of all those warts on your hands. They must all have gone away completely."

I had been plagued by warts for a long time, occasionally making some effort to treat them but never meeting with the slightest success. Now I really had to cure myself – and quickly! Our local pharmacist gave me a phial labelled "Arg. Nitr." (silver nitrate) which I was to apply diligently twice a day. It hurt terribly but did destroy the warts right down to their roots. I was a proud and happy girl when the day came at last that they had all finally disappeared. Nothing now could stand in the way of my great adventure.

So there were three of us who set off in high spirits for Edinburgh that late autumn of 1869 – Will, Nellie and me. We were to stay in a little flat in Duke Street containing a dining room, a living room and a single bedroom for Will. Nellie and I slept upstairs in a small attic. The arrangement worked well, with Will of course in complete charge: his word was law to us two girls and no disagreements whatsoever were allowed. The first task was to find me a school but that was quite simple as Nellie already had attended a good private school there. All the children in my class were between ten and twelve years old so that I fitted in nicely, being placed in the middle group. Our teacher was a kindly man but so enormously fat that he could barely squeeze through the classroom door, to our great amusement. He drove to school each day in a pony cart which, it was said, had been specially built to carry his weight, the previous one having reputedly collapsed under the strain.

To begin with, going to school and being away from home for the very first time was a daunting experience and I felt very timid at being a country child suddenly thrust in amongst a crowd of city girls who all seemed so sophisticated and well-dressed. I was certain they must despise me for having only the plainest of home-made woollen dresses to wear. But gradually I settled down and grew steadily more confident. I enjoyed the work and was soon able to impress the headmaster, who gave us religious instruction, by my knowledge of the Bible. In other respects, however, it was quite hard to catch up with the others, especially starting midway through the term and having therefore missed a great deal.

For English literature we were expected to read *The Seasons* by James Thomson, preparing a large chunk of this massive poem every day. When I arrived, the class had struggled as far as "Autumn" and the whole rigmarole seemed to me the most arid and tedious piece of literature imaginable. That evening I was busy doing my homework seated at our work table in the living-room and was growing increasingly tired of Thomson's high-flown but interminable descriptions of Nature when I was suddenly struck by some lines that I didn't understand. Thomson had been waxing lyrical about harvest time but then began to describe the wonders of personified "Industry" who showed Man

How to raise
His feeble force by the mechanic powers.

"Please help me, Will," I said. "What does Thomson mean by "mechanic powers?"

Now Will, like his father, nearly always insisted that I should find things out for myself. This time, though, he took pity on me – maybe simply because he was so interested in the subject of mechanics. On top of all his theological studies, he was then working at the University as assistant to Professor Peter Tait of the Natural Philosophy Department and the whole subject seemed to be taking up more and more of his attention.

So we sat together for more than an hour while he gently told me all about what was meant by those mysterious "mechanical powers". Some of it, at least, I began to understand. Next day, the English class was proceeding in its usual placid way. It was in fact only my third day there. Our teacher came to the very lines that had puzzled me. "What does our poet mean by 'mechanic powers?" he asked a girl in the lowest stream. No answer was forthcoming. His cane was pointed towards the next pupil and then directed with increasing impatience along every row at each girl in turn until he reached the top group. Still no reply came and it was clear to us all that none would be forthcoming. I sat shaking with trepidation. This was, I realised, a perfect opportunity to upstage the others, yet my mouth was dry and I felt I wouldn't be able to utter a word. Obviously our teacher noticed my agitation and steered his cane straight towards me, raising his eyebrows simultaneously.

Summoning up all the courage I possessed, I blurted out, "Levers and cranes and . . . pulleys and . . ."

Then I dried up. I knew lots more but not a word would come.

"Quite correct," said our teacher approvingly. "And can you give us some more examples, Miss Smith?"

"K-k-keystone and wedge, sir," I stammered at length. After that my mind became a blank. But it had been enough. At the end of the week, everyone moved places, as was the custom, and I picked up my books and went, as I understood, to take my place at the top of the class."

But the girl who sat haughtily there hissed scornfully, "Not here, you ass! You're only top of the middle group."

I still had lots to learn in all kinds of way. I was buoyed up at having made an obvious impression so soon on pupils and teachers alike but the expectations on me increased all the more. Will had written home telling the family about my success and they too seemed to expect I would stay at the top. I began working like a Trojan now, but it wasn't always enough. I started to move up steadily but the brightest girl in the class – the one who had hissed at me – was absolutely determined not to lose her place and a fierce though not unfriendly rivalry developed between us. One week, however, I was dismayed and ashamed to find I had slipped back several places, in spite of all my efforts.

At last I confided in Will one night when Nellie was out visiting. "I feel such a failure, Willie. I'm letting all of you down but I simply can't manage to stay top of the class all of the time."

"Of course you can," he said. "Just keep at it. If I can do it, so can you."

"No, no, Will. That's just the problem. *You* can do it. Everybody knows that. You find everything so easy. But I don't. Remember, I've never had real school lessons before. All these other girls, they've been going to proper school for years. They know the system inside out. I don't. There are still so many gaps in my knowledge and I don't believe I'll ever catch up."

Will's answer was a strange one. "All right, Alice, I understand that. But I still know you can do it. All it needs it more effort. This is what we'll do. I know you love butter. Well, we'll make it a rule from now on that you can only have butter if you've had a successful week at school. Drop a place – no butter. Gain a place – butter every day for a week."

Mother regularly sent us a tub of salted butter through the winter months. It wasn't that I relished it particularly (I preferred my butter unsalted) but I felt deeply hurt by Will's apparent harshness. What he understood as an inducement I saw as a punishment. My appetite, never good at the best of times, faded away still more and my general health began to suffer on the meagre diet of bread and jam. I couldn't complain openly – after all, I knew that Will was paying all the school fees and living expenses for both Nellie and me there out of his prize money and his earnings from working for Professor Tait. But when Mother learned about Will's sanctions, she was quite angry with him and said it would have to stop. And so it did.

Fortunately the struggle at school was not nearly as hopeless as I'd feared. Slowly I pulled myself up again, especially as I came to know the other girls better. The fight to be *dux* of the class at the end of the whole year was intense but not at all bitter or spiteful. After New Year, we began swotting for our exams and I spent every free moment with my head bowed over history and geography textbooks till I had everything off by heart, whether or not I properly understood what I had read. That seemed to me to be the only right way to learn. I had never sat written tests before and the thought of them began to panic me.

When the day of the first exam arrived and I sat down at the desk, my whole mind seemed to become a complete jumble. It was a history paper and I could scarcely read the questions at first because my eyes wouldn't focus properly. Facts that I knew perfectly well seemed to have vanished out of my head. Even so, I began to write feverishly and went on until we were all told to put down our pens. Next day came a geography exam and I went through the same agonising performance.

When the results were announced a few days later, my marks turned out to be the best in the class, to my total astonishment. Will of course was delighted and immediately wrote home with the good news. All he said to me though was: "I told you so, Alice, didn't I?"

Now it was openly predicted by the other girls at school that I would certainly end up top of the class in June. But they didn't know, as I did, that I might not still be in Edinburgh then. Will's final year at New College would finish at Easter and by the January of 1870 it was an open secret that he meant to apply for the vacant Chair of Hebrew at Aberdeen Free Church College, provided he could muster enough support .

Though Will had warned Nellie and me not to mention the matter to anyone, I was well aware that both Father and Will's closest friend in Edinburgh, Tom Lindsay, were busily canvassing on his behalf throughout the Free Church congregations. Will himself had written to all the eminent professors he had met in Germany asking for testimonials on his behalf. He knew that he could easily stay on in Edinburgh because Professor Tait had repeatedly said how much he needed Will's help in setting up the new physics laboratory at the University; but since childhood my brother's heart had been set on serving the Free Church. No one and nothing, he asserted, would dissuade him from that goal.

It was all very sad and miserable for me. While no formal appointment could be made until the General Assembly met in May, I had the gloomy conviction that my Edinburgh days were coming to an end – just as I was beginning to enjoy myself at school, gaining in confidence day by day, and finding more and more satisfaction in studying. It was all so different from the very predictable and rather dull routine of life at home. Nellie and I had made lots of friends in Edinburgh in spite of Will's strict rule was that we could only go out visiting on Saturdays. The two of us also loved sight-seeing: we climbed right to the top of the Scott Monument and went to Holyrood House to see where poor Mary Queen of Scots had lived and where her lover Rizzio had been murdered in front of her eyes. The dark patches on the staircase, so the guide assured us, were the very bloodstains marking the awful deed to this day.

It was bitterly cold in Edinburgh that winter and there

were some dreadful storms – one that I still remember vividly brought such a hurricane that I would have been blown right into the path of a cab in the street if Will hadn't grabbed hold of me just in time. We hadn't gone home for Christmas that year, partly because of the cost, partly because the long, unheated train journey would have been a nightmare. Our social life though made up for that. Nellie and I had become friendly with Tom Lindsay's sister and we all went often for afternoon tea.

At New Year, we were offered something very rich and fruity called "black bun" which I'd never tasted before:. Our hosts saw that Nell and I thought it wonderful and said, "Do come again soon and finish it. Tom won't touch it, you know."

Nellie wanted to go back the next day but I felt that would be rude. So we put it off for a whole week. But when we returned, confidently expecting to finish the black bun, there was not the slightest mention of it. Either the family had eaten it or had forgotten all about their offer!

Meantime, a fortnight before, Professor Tait and his wife had invited us all for a Christmas Eve meal at their fine, large house in Drummond Place. Will had often been to the Tait's home but this was the first visit there for Nellie and me and neither of us had ever tasted a traditional Christmas dinner. We had read, of course, about such things as mince-pies and plum-pudding, but had never actually seen such a spread of delicacies in all our lives. For us, the highlight of the meal was the plum-pudding, decorated with a sprig of holly and carried shoulder-high to the table in a blue glow of flaming brandy. Father would most gravely have disapproved had he known about it. The whole experience was wonderful, yet I was far too shy on that first visit to enjoy myself properly and felt relieved to come home again to our small flat.

Mrs Tait, however, was determined to persevere with us and the next thing we knew an invitation arrived for the two of us girls to accompany her to a pantomime starring a famous magician of the day who called himself *The Wizard of the North*. I had, of course, never been inside a theatre and sat there utterly spellbound as one amazing illusion followed another.

I don't remember much about the performance now, except that he placed a suitcase on the table and then produced from it a stream of curious objects, one after another, until the stage floor was covered. Finally, with a great flourish, his daughter jumped out of the suitcase to thunderous applause from the audience. Then he shook the sleeves of his silk blouse and a whole swarm of butterflies emerged. Mrs Tait was so pleased by our evident delight that she offered to take us to another theatrical performance the following week. But at first Will drew the line at more entertainment of that kind.

"I'm truly sorry, Alice," he said, "but I can't take the risk. My chances of the Aberdeen thing" – that was how he always spoke of the prospective professorship – "would be absolutely ruined if it got about that my sisters were attending profane performances in an Edinburgh theatre. Apart from that, our parents would be horrified if they learned about it."

Certainly I knew vaguely that theatres were supposed to be very sinful places, full of temptations of one kind or another, though what form those temptations actually took I had no idea. I was prepared to take a chance. "Do ask them anyway," I pleaded, knowing the faith that both Mother and Father placed in him.

Will gave way at last, perhaps much more because of his relationship with the Taits than for our sakes. He sent a telegram home and, much to my surprise, parental permission was forthcoming. "Only this once," had been the terse condition attached by Father – for we all knew the story of one eminent Free Kirk minister whose son had become an actor, and whose name ever after could only be uttered with bated breath. Nothing, it was made clear, could be allowed to jeopardise Will's chances of getting that Hebrew chair at Aberdeen.

So Nell and I went off again to the theatre with kindly Mrs Tait, this time to see *Ali Baba and the Forty Thieves*. If anything, the pantomime was more wonderful than the *Wizard of the North* had been. We were thrilled by the music, the spectacle and the knockabout comedy. Quite probably there was a good deal of repartee that I didn't altogether understand; even so, these shows had given me glimpses into another world – a fantasy land of light and laughter, where nothing was entirely predictable and where mystery and magic coloured everything. When term began again, it seemed very hard to return to a life of study but Will made it plain to us both that it had to be done and so we gradually returned to the old familiar habits of sobriety and steady industry.

Will normally went straight home to Keig as soon as the College term ended just before Easter. This time though he was anxious to stay on in Edinburgh at least until the Aberdeen appointment was decided one way or another. I had high hopes therefore of being able to remain at school and maybe even to gain the dux prize for the year. But things were to turn out very differently.

It all began with a climb up Arthur's Seat, that magnificent lion's back of a hill that overlooks the whole of Edinburgh, with the Castle to the west and the whole length of the Firth of Forth to the north and east. A friend of Nellie accompanied us and the three of us set off in high spirits one bright but cold Saturday morning in March. Halfway up I suddenly began to turn faint with all the exertion; then the bitter east wind quickly chilled me to the bone. I felt utterly ashamed of myself, someone after all who thought nothing of climbing up Cairn William, but at last I had to give up. The other two found a sheltered niche for me out of the wind.

"Look, Alice," said Nellie, "We'll run up to the top to see the view, then come straight back for you."

And so they did, in less than half an hour. I still felt queasy but going down was much easier than the climb. Better still, we stopped at a baker's shop on the way home and bought three hot mutton pies: they tasted as delicious as anything I had ever eaten and by the time we reached our lodgings I felt fine again. As usual, we'd been invited out for tea that afternoon but now it was Nellie's turn to be out of sorts, complaining that she had the most terrible headache. Next day she was worse and had a high fever. Will sent for the doctor who was unsure of the diagnosis but muttered something about the possibility of scarlet fever, which put us all in the most frightful panic.

Will immediately sent off a telegram to Keig and by late next day Mother had arrived to take charge of the patient. We all felt greatly relieved. I was to stay with our friends, Dr and Mrs Brackenridge, so that Will could still have his own room – by now he was utterly exhausted and looking quite ill himself. It had become clear though that Nellie had caught a bad dose of mumps, not scarlet fever, so her life was not considered to be in danger any longer.

Once the crisis was over, Mother turned her attention to me, "You're looking quite dreadful, so skinny! Surely you're not eating enough!" she said bluntly. "Your skin is grey. Maybe it's all the reek in this Edinburgh air. That's it, Alice. You haven't been washing yourself properly. Come here at once and let me scrub your face." I had to consent but felt humiliated to be treated as if I was a child again and not a young lady of nearly twelve. Finally, Mother expresses herself satisfied.

"There we are, bairn. I can see the colour in your cheeks again." But of course she knew, just as I did, that it was simply a result of her vigorous rubbing, not to mention my angry blushes. And then, as Nellie gradually grew better, I began to have more stabbing pains in my back, which I put down at first to an unpleasant incident when, on my way to school, a rough baker's boy had mischievously swung his big basket at me, hitting me hard between the shoulders. I thought nothing of it at the time but later that evening such a spasm of pain went through me that I could hardly move. So now it was my turn to be exhibited to the Doctor for his opinion.

"She'll be far better off at home, Mrs Smith," Dr Brackenridge pronounced dogmatically. "Back at Keig and up there in your clean country air she'll be as right as rain. Auld Reekie's no place for this young lady with its windy streets and all those chimneys spewing out soot day and night. A change of air is what she needs! Take her back with you."

All my hopes of staying on at school in Edinburgh were instantly dashed. Mother had to go home as soon as possible and there was to be no last minute reprieve. I had time only for one quick visit to the school to say goodbye to the headmaster.

"We'll miss you greatly, Alice my dear," he said. "You made such a valuable contribution to my religious education class – and to the other classes too. Really, I don't know what we shall do without you. You were shaping up to become as talented as your brother William. Indeed you were!"

That last comment, no doubt sincerely meant, only twisted the knife all the more.

Private   Privatissimum

MISS A. Smith

PRIVATE

Aberdeen - 25th Nov

My dear Alice

By Prussian I suppose you mean German peasants — well their dress varies. The men generally wear long blue smock-frocks coming half way down the thigh — any sort of trousers they can get, & little round caps with none in front. So [illegible]. In some places they wear knee breeches however — I think there are [illegible] of some German peasants of a more picturesque kind in Mamma's album. The women's dress varies more — blue frocks are I think commonest; in some places however the frock is very short not much if anything past the knees so as to show white stockings & bright gaiters — in this case there is also an apron with a body and the dress is square & low in front showing a thick white chemisette high at the neck.

Moreover in this dress all the hair is gathered up into a high knot at the back of the head — dragged back from the face & ears & topped by a little black silk cap or rather cushion. N.B. not a chignon but a top-knot — the hair on all sides pulled up to the top.

In other parts the dress is generally long enough — the apron has no body, no cap is worn but the hair plaited behind with a bodkin to hold it. The bodkin is like the blade of a breakfast knife but often gilt generally. Or a little embroidered cap just reaching from ear to ear goes over the back — not the top of the head.

The men do not wear a smock frock, they wear a looped jacket — like what char: wear nearly — but rather fuller. Generally it is grey with

green edging & even a green collar; and generally two buttons are put at the back with a little strap of the green edged cloth between them. To conclude the features of the subject.

What will you send for? A pincushion?

Small cap. Back & head-piece. Painter.

You owe me 4 letters. Farewell this [illegible]

12. A letter written by Will to Alice from Germany in 1871

13. One of Alice's numerous drawings

potato-vine (solanacaea)

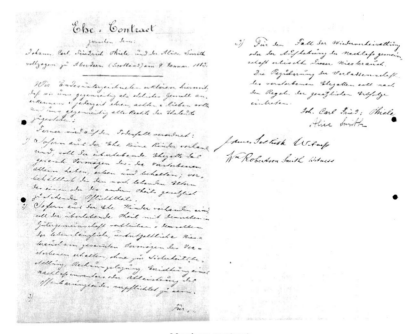

Marriage contract
between Johann Carl Friedrich Thiele and Alice Smith,
executed at Aberdeen on January 9, 1883.

We the undersigned herewith declare that we mutually consent to entering into the bond of matrimony as husband and wife, desiring to honour, respect and love one another at all times and jointly accepting the rights and duties of marriage.

In the event of death, it is decreed that:

In the absence of any offspring to the marriage, the surviving spouse shall inherit the entire estate of the deceased and retain sole rights to the estate, apart from the legal portion due to the surviving parents of either partner.

Where there are offspring of the marriage, the surviving partner shall enjoy a life interest in the property together with the right of permanent occupancy, free of all encumbrances, without the rendering of accounts, the drawing up of an inventory or the completion of an affidavit of means.

In the case of a second marriage or of the dissolution of the estate, such rights will cease to exist and the inheritance laws shall apply to the deceased's estate, according to the rules of intestacy.

Joh.Carl Friedr. Thiele
Alice Smith

James Selkirk Witness
Wm. Robertson Smith Witness

14. Alice's marriage-contract, drawn up by Will and a translation

15. A page out of Alice's manuscript, with a sketch of the inclined plane

Turning to Butterflies

When we reached home that Easter of 1870, Mother was the first to fall sick, having caught the mumps from nursing Nellie in Edinburgh. Then each one of us picked it up in turn, with the result that the next few weeks were decidedly miserable for the whole family. On top of everything else, my own recovery was slow and those mysterious stabbing pains in my spine returned with a vengeance. Whatever their cause, the back trouble was now so bad that I could scarcely sit upright on a chair and ended up spending most of the time lying on the floor. Our kind-hearted maid helped by massaging my back whenever I could sneak through to the kitchen without Mother noticing. To my surprise I also discovered that a long walk in the countryside did wonders to ease the ache and even Mother, completely sceptical at first, eventually admitted, "Well, I must say the walking seems to do you no harm, Alice. And I must say it's a wonderful treatment that lets you go and do parish visits on Papa's behalf!"

I had now turned twelve. In May, Will was successfully elected to the Hebrew chair at Aberdeen Free College and so Father naturally attended the General Assembly in Edinburgh where the appointment was formally announced. Both he and Will were congratulated on all sides and Father wrote joyfully home to Mother: "It is marvellous how much satisfaction Willie's election has given to the whole Church. Have we not cause for great thankfulness?"

Will had at first meant to make a European tour that summer of 1870 with his close friend, John Black, who was teaching for a short time at a college in Seville but the outbreak of the Franco-Prussian was to put a stop to that plan. Instead he went off for a short holiday at Braemar and I was just happy to know he would soon be back with us. The very fact that Will would be living in Aberdeen and close at hand was the most important thing. It made up for the sadness of my departure from Edinburgh and the abandonment of my budding school career. Who knows what I might have ended up doing? Those were exciting times for women – in 1869 Sophia Jex-Blake and four other women had at last been allowed to begin studying medicine at Edinburgh University and Nellie and I had discussed this very eagerly, though I think our parents would not altogether have approved of women's rights being extended that far. In those days most of our own sex would not have trusted a lady doctor. But Will seemed to feel it was the right way forward; after all, he had helped Professor Tait run the "Ladies' classes" in natural philosophy and he used to remark that their work was often far better than that of the male students, for all that they were not allowed to graduate.

My education at home began once more and, wisely or not, Father decided I should start to learn Latin for a second time under his guidance. The first attempt had been away back in 1866 when I was only eight and now, four years later, Father suddenly announced in his peremptory way: "We'll begin Latin again, Alice, right from page one!" At that time I disagreed vehemently with the idea but it was typical of his teaching approach and looking back I feel he was probably right. Even so, progress was still painfully slow and I found the job of relearning all the tables of declensions and conjugations very tiresome indeed.

On the other hand, the rote learning did ensure that the basics of Latin were firmly fixed in my mind for all time. Only when I had mastered the grammar through and through did Father hand me my first Latin reader – a small book called *Dilectus*. Later on I tackled Caesar's *De Bello Gallico*, together with parts of Ovid and Virgil. I especially loved the *Aeneid* with its resonant hexameters.

Considered now to be a sensible and relatively deserving student in Father's eyes, I was allowed henceforth to do all my work in his study, which as you know served also as dining room and living room outwith school hours. During the morning, however, the room was holy ground, to be entered on tiptoe and only by those privileged to work there. Not even Mother would have dreamt of coming in unasked at that time of day. All the boarding students were boys so I was conscious of being exceptionally favoured and I suppose Father must have thought me bright enough to justify this radical break with tradition and convention. Perhaps he had after all been influenced by the growing demand for equal educational rights for women!

In the schoolroom, every pupil began the day with Latin or Greek, having prepared it more or less diligently the evening before. Father listened to each student's translation in turn and discussed any difficult points thoroughly. But, just as happened in the family devotions, if anyone stumbled over their translation of a prepared passage, he immediately showed his irritation by a brusque command of "Get on! Get on with you!"

When that lesson was over, we all sat around the big table for mathematics. I enjoyed this particularly because I had quite a flair for calculation and found the basics relatively easy to grasp. It helped too that it was Father's favourite subject and he took great pleasure in setting us complicated numerical puzzles of one kind or another as a challenge.

Eventually he announced that I was ready to tackle geometry but I soon found myself completely lost in the complexities of Euclid and complained, "Oh, Papa, I'm finding this very hard! Truly I am."

Father's typically laconic response was simply, "If ye canna dae it, ye'll hae to gie it up, for I'll no waste time on ye." And so geometry was abandoned.

Instead I was to begin algebra. This time I was to do it all on my own. "You'll hae to work it out for yourself," he admonished. "Come to me only if you must."

This time though he added a quite unexpected inducement: "If you get through the first twenty exercises, Alice, wi'oot ony help frae me, I'll find you the money to buy thon clock you've always wanted."

This was a real incentive because I had been desperate to have a clock for our old nursery wall. In any case, the example set by my elder brothers, George and Will, was enough to spur me on. Why, after all, should they be smarter than me?

Father attached great importance to clear, well-formed legible handwriting (perhaps because his own was never good) and so copybook exercises also figured largely in the daily routine. What we copied out was completely irrelevant and I enjoyed the task so much that I began to embellish my work – mostly extracts from my favourite poetry book, Macaulay's *Lays of Ancient Rome* – with intricate little scrolls and curlicues for which I was sternly reprimanded. If, declared Father, I had the time to scribble away like that, it was a sure sign I was being sinfully idle! The artistic streak on Mother's side of the family found no echo in my father's breast.

Fortunately Father paid little or no attention to what happened outside his study and so I was free to draw as much as I liked in the nursery. Lucy and Nellie both joined me in this hobby and we literally papered the wall of the room with our pictures. As soon as the drawings on one wall began to look tattered, we stripped them off and began all over again with a fresh collection. Illustrated magazines were then just coming into fashion and since our Aberdeen friends were generous in passing these on we had any amount of material to copy from. This turned out to be an ideal way of passing the time on many a wet afternoon at the Manse of Keig.

At first we mostly copied geometric patterns and ornamental borders. Then a Mr Bruce from Banff, one of Father's old students, came to stay for a weekend, admired our drawings and said, "I'll see if I can find you something more interesting to draw." He was as good as his word and in a week or so there arrived a heavy parcel with two large folios containing the most beautiful set of lithographs – pictures of trees, landscapes and stately homes – and with those for our models we began to broaden our artistic horizons. But I still knew nothing at all of Scottish art and artists.

As I explained earlier, it was arranged that two girls of about our own ages should come and join Lucy and me in Mother's lessons, partly for the sake of their own education but also to provide us with some outside company. They spent the whole of each weekday with us and so we enjoyed many pleasant afternoons together in the garden or out walking. Now, while I was customarily the only girl allowed to study with Father, he unexpectedly took the notion of teaching all four of us some English grammar, a subject that had always been conspicuously absent from the manse curriculum. He produced a small, old-fashioned primer of English grammar and declared he would take us all for a short lesson every morning directly after family assembly. We would work together as a little class of four, not individually, and every week we would be ranked by merit, just as had been the custom at my school in Edinburgh. Moreover, Father announced he would award a prize to the best girl pupil at the end of the session. She would be *dux* and her reward was to be a most elegant pen-knife with two blades and a mother-of-pearl handle – certainly a very appealing inducement to me.

One of the two girls, Ann, was at least a year older than me and intellectually very bright, though she lacked my experience of schooling as well as my thorough grounding in the basic skills. So the two of us were close rivals and I had to make some genuine effort to stay top of the little class. The youngest girl, Louisa, posed no challenge and my sister Lucy, who always seemed a scatter-brain at that age, showed no outward interest in education, being happiest when roaming around outside with the animals. By the time we had reached the last but still very elementary exercise in the grammar book, I was growing frankly bored with the whole business and thought it time we had some fun. The exercise in question was made up of a long list of sentences each containing a grammatical error. Taking it in turns, we were to read out a sentence and then correct it as fast as we could. If any of us made a slip, Father seemed to take delight in bawling "Wrong!" in a thunderous tone. For some reason the errors were all ridiculously simple – a typical example might have been: *Mary is always obedient to his parents.* We were expected of course to alter *his* to *her* but boldly I proposed to change the subject of the sentence instead.

"Look, if we say, 'John is always obedient to his parents,' that will still be perfectly correct grammatically and Father won't be able to say, 'Wrong!' will he? The others were distinctly uneasy about this daring scheme and Louisa plaintively remarked, "But you know fine the Doctor will simply cry, 'Wrong!' and turn to the next one of us for the right answer."

"We only have to agree, all four of us, that we give *exactly* the same answer," I insisted, thinking myself very cunning. "Then he's *bound* to admit that we're right."

So they reluctantly agreed to join in this very risky jape. I was first and read out: *The Queen made a rousing speech to his troops at Tilbury.*

Without a pause I went on: "That should read, *The King made a rousing speech to his troops at Tilbury*".

Father gave me a withering look and roared, "Wrong! Next" – pointing to Ann, who would dearly have liked to show me up, yet who had seemed more willing than either Lucy or Louisa to join in the game. She hesitated, gulped, turned bright red, and then her courage deserting her, blurted out, "It should say, sir, *The Queen made a rousing speech to her troops at Tilbury*."

"Right!" shouted Father in his most schoolmasterly tones, "Go to the top of the class, Ann. As for you, Alice, we shall be greatly honoured to have no such classroom frivolity in future."

I was absolutely furious, not just at losing my place but at being convicted wrongly of not knowing the simplest of English grammar.

In the end though I easily won my coveted pen-knife prize and spent ages happily carving little wooden dolls, animals and dolls' furniture with it. Then one day I found to my horror that the knife had disappeared from the apron pocket where I guarded it jealously. Closer investigation showed that a tiny hole in the pocket was responsible – and sadly the knife never reappeared.

* * * *

By this time the old nursery had long since been transformed into our girls' common-room and there, as you know, we spent most winter afternoons, mostly all by ourselves, though Mother still kept a careful eye on everything we did and continued to give us the kind of training she thought suitable for young ladies of our station in life. It was she too who continued to teach us religious education, history and of course some geography once again, after her failed attempt to turn Bella into our pupil-teacher. Every day we also did our prescribed share of needlework. Other subjects that are open nowadays to any girl – art, literature and the sciences – were considered by Mother to be neither necessary nor indeed proper for young ladies.

Yet in many respects both our parents would have thought themselves decidedly advanced in their views on how girls should be educated and I believe they had no fundamental objection to our learning as much as possible. But their time and resources were limited and Father' priority was without any doubt the coaching of his sons and the boarding students.

We were all encouraged to read widely for the sake of broadening our general knowledge but the range of books available to us in those days was distinctly limited. Father's own library was now becoming extensive, thanks to Will, but was far too technical for any of us, while fiction very seldom came our way, being considered frivolous and time-wasting at best and at worst capable of exerting a decidedly harmful influence on the minds of impressionable young ladies. To Father's delight, Will could now afford to bring him all manner of expensive scientific and theological treatises but Will himself never overcame the influence of his parents' prejudice against novel reading and would only read fiction when his doctor actually prescribed that as an antidote for "overwork".

I remember Will finding me out in the garden one summer's day deeply immersed in reading *his* copy of George Eliot's *Middlemarch*, a book I thought wonderful in its portrayal of character. I hardly ever saw my brother really angry but on this occasion he seemed quite carried away with indignation. He had just finished reading *Middlemarch* himself – "purely as a duty," he said – and it was no fit book for any of his sisters to read!

"*Middlemarch!*" he snorted derisively. "It's a thoroughly bad book. In the first place it's bad art. Why should that woman's characters need a whole commentary to tell us *why* they're acting the way they do. I can't stand that psychological anatomising. Shakespeare didn't need to do it, did he? Shakespeare just gave us the characters and allowed us to draw our own conclusions. These modern 'anatomical' novels are every bit as abominable as those modern painters who seem determined to prove they know all about the bones and muscles underneath the skin! It's almost indecent."

I was only sixteen at the time and didn't dare argue, even though I disagreed totally with what Will seemed to be saying. For me, it was all-important to know just *why* Dorothea Brooke felt and acted as she did. I regarded her as a female hero!

But I plucked up enough courage to say, "Why did you read it yourself then?"

For a moment he was hesitated, then answered quietly: "Because my doctor prescribed it, that's why. And I may say was a bitter medicine for me! I could hardly stomach it."

He paused a moment and then, seeing my doubtful glance, went on. "As it happens, I've been writing to my friend Black about *Middlemarch*. *He* thought it was excellent. But I've told him *I* feel it's morally bad; maybe not altogether wicked, but it's quite wrong for a woman novelist to show her readers so very hollow and false a world. She ought to try to be more uplifting. The whole lesson of the book seems to be that the world is without any moral unity or purpose at all. It's my belief that the fellow she lives with – George Lewes – is responsible for leading her astray and giving her those unhealthy, morbid ideas. I really don't understand why everyone raves about *Middlemarch*. Dickens' novels have the same vulgarity. In her case it's only a slightly more refined vulgarity!"

I was sure Will must in some way be right – because we took it for granted that he always *was* right – and so I thought my pleasure in reading George Eliot must be somehow wicked or sinful. Moreover, my brother had mentioned that George Eliot "lived with that fellow Lewes" – whatever he meant by that – and in a mysterious way it was clear to me that even reading a book by George Eliot, let alone writing such a novel, must truly be wicked as well as exciting.

That caused me a great deal of heart-searching at the time and left me with feelings of guilt for many years. As Mary Jane had written short stories before she died, I couldn't help fancying that in some awful way she had perhaps been punished by God. On the other hand, I nowadays realise that Will's own outlook became in many ways more liberal once he had been dismissed from his post in Aberdeen and was acquiring an ever-widening circle of friends in London, Cambridge and abroad. Already he had begun to bring us reading material that he thought suited to our female tastes whenever he came home for the weekend from Aberdeen during the seventies. Those included Lewis Carroll's *Alice* books, which even delighted Father because of their mathematical problems and paradoxes!

Large illustrated magazines such as *Sunday at Home* and *Leisure Hour* had always been allowed in the manse and were read eagerly by all of us. *Sunday at Home* was naturally reserved for the Sabbath while *Leisure Hour* kept us going for the remaining six days. Eventually the manse library boasted a long line of bound volumes of these magazines, side by side with Father's austere and unreadable theological journals. The boys ridiculed our magazines though and threatened to have them thrown out to make way for new scientific periodicals such as *Nature* which they and Father now devoured greedily.

My own favourite reading place on warm summer days was the broad, comfortable bough of a beech tree at the edge of the woods. There, in my early teens, I began my long acquaintance with Scott, Dickens and Thackeray. Scott was my favourite author and I took every chance of borrowing any novel of his that I hadn't yet read. Reading Scott was strictly an occupation for the school holidays, however, because once I had begun one of his romances it caught hold of me, heart and soul, and I could think of little else until the book was finished. *Waverley* was my introduction to Scott and I was in tears by the time I came to the hero's tragic end in the final pages.

Then I heard Mother's voice calling, "Alice, Alice! Where are you? I need you". As soon as I had clambered down from my perch and run to meet her, she saw that I'd been crying.

"What has come over you, lass? Whatever's wrong now?"

"Nothing, Mamma, nothing at all. It's just that I've been reading *Waverley* and the ending's so sad."

She put her arm comfortingly round my shoulder. "Alice, my dearest, it's only a story. Not real life, you know. You mustn't take stories to heart like that. Papa wouldn't like it. He'd stop you reading such books if he knew you were affected by them so much."

That really frightened me. But Mother never mentioned the matter again. I was so voracious a reader that I tackled anything at all, no matter what the subject was or how tattered the book.

One of our most respected parishioners, a leading elder, once presented me with a book by Hugh Miller – *The Old Red Sandstone* – which provided my first insights into geology and palaeontology, even though I found parts of it quite difficult. Miller had been a notable and staunch supporter of the Free Church ever since the 1843 Disruption but his scientific work and his publications had brought him under increasing suspicion by the Kirk and by the time of his death in 1856, he was beginning to be regarded in some Kirk quarters as distinctly "unsound". The fact that he ultimately committed suicide served only to confirm the belief amongst some that Miller's rash investigations into the Creator's handiwork had brought God's just condemnation upon him.

Odd indeed it was that I'd been given *The Old Red Sandstone* to read in 1873 just three years before my brother's own writings were to split our Free Church into opposing camps. Stranger still that the Kirk elder from whom I got the book turned out to be the fiercest opponent in our parish of Will's fight for the freedom to read the Bible critically. All these matters gave me food for anxious thought as I grew older.

My own reading went on apace. Father gave me a leather-bound copy of Lamb's *Tales from Shakespeare* which I treasured and he encouraged me to build up my own library with works like Macaulay's *History of England*, Robinson's *History of America* (now long-forgotten) and Prescott's *Conquest of Mexico*. My sisters were less addicted to reading apart from Nellie, but all of us enjoyed reading poetry aloud in the nursery – though Byron's work was banned!

The twelve months after Aunt Mattie left us and before Nellie went off to Germany with Will hold precious memories for me. Though she and Bella were so much older than Lucy and I, the elder girls no longer treated us as children and we were now all young women together, the old nursery our undisputed private domain where we sat, sewed, chatted and shared harmless little romances as a way of bringing some imaginary excitement into the uniformity of our otherwise quiet and uneventful lives.

It was a sign that we were all now growing into young women that one of our favourite games was the bantering exchange of fanciful notions about potential local admirers for one another − local lads we knew slightly but whom our parents would of course have regarded as totally unsuitable marital prospects for a minister's daughters. As my particular prospective lover, my sisters all agreed teasingly on one young but rather *dour* farmer's son. They picked him solely on the basis that his mother had once remarked to Mother, at the church door: "Oh, Mistress Smith, oor Sandy says he'd like fine to sit in the Kirk the hale day, just looking at your Alice's bonny fair hair."

That was enough for them to concoct an elaborate imaginary romance between Sandy and me which they then embroidered wildly from day to day. I joined happily in the game and gave as good as I got. But Nellie's departure put an end to those amusements and when she returned home after thirteen months in Germany she was engaged herself and took the matter of marriage far more seriously. Ellen Dean (that was her full baptismal name) was a lively, strong character and highly sociable; she loved music and art equally and became more proficient than any of the rest of us as both a pianist and amateur artist. I am sure that she, far more than Lucy and I, inherited her painting skills from our grand-uncle, James Giles.

In the summer of 1872, Will invited Nellie to accompany him to Germany when he went back to Göttingen for further study with his favourite theologian, Ritschl, and to undertake the study of Arabic under Paul Lagarde. Nellie herself studied music and German, while also enjoying the varied social life there, so much so that in July Will wrote home, "Nellie has got so well acquainted in the town that I propose she shall stay here through the winter in the home of a retired minister, Pastor Koch."

But Will himself went touring the Bavarian Alps with his friend, the eminent mathematician Felix Klein, before returning to Aberdeen, and in the meantime Nellie had made the acquaintance of another young student, Gerhard, the son of a minister and heir to a large and prosperous farm near Würzburg. A secret romance between the pair quickly blossomed and the first any of the family heard of the matter was when Nellie herself wrote in December asking permission to move to Würzburg. That suggestion at once alarmed Father who regarded the town as a hotbed of Catholicism. And his consternation grew worse once it emerged that Nellie was in love – claiming indeed to be engaged! Both parents insisted she come home as once. Of course she obeyed; but continued the relationship by letter. Gerhard's own parents were quite opposed to the idea of their son marrying a foreigner but he nevertheless insisted to Nellie that he would set about building a house for them both. He began the project indeed and was visited by Will on whom he made a favourable impression. Yet in the end nothing came of it all and he never made the promised journey to visit Nellie in Scotland. In those circumstances it was inevitable that the affair gradually withered and died – but it was a long and painful three years for my sister. Her hair turned grey in that time and, though she remained the same kind, patient and loving sister that she had always been, she grew very serious and completely lost her youthful vivacity.

Will thought it good for Nellie to have work to distract her and arranged for her to translate a German theological work into English – a labour for which she was paid adequately. In addition, Lucy and I began to have regular lessons in music and German from her. It was during this weary time too that I went off for a few months to stay in Aberdeen with Will, partly to improve my French through daily tuition from a Mlle Boudon, who had a first-class reputation as a teacher. Though I enjoyed having Will's company, I made few friends in the city and found life there fairly lonesome until Lucy joined me briefly. Our old fellow-pupil at Keig, Ann, was also boarding in Aberdeen by that time and the three of us would team up for long walks. As ever, Will always worried if we came home late and typically would fly into a temper with us – just as he used to do in Edinburgh whenever Nellie didn't arrive home promptly. Like father, like son, again.

My health continued to give me much pain and anxiety. Ever since my stay in Edinburgh, I had suffered intermittently from the back pains I described earlier and, though outdoor exercise helped greatly, bending so much over books while studying seemed to make the condition worse. As far as possible I tried to ignore the problem, or at least to avoid drawing attention to it because I knew Mother would worry. Above all I feared both parents would try to stop me studying and that was something not to be contemplated. So I soldiered on, often slipping quietly into the kitchen to get our maid to massage my back while I lay flat on the table there. Continuing to play the piano on cold mornings was especially stupid of me.

So I relied mostly on my regular walks to keep me fit and this gave both Father and Mother the illusion that all was well. Seeing what he regarded simply as a natural pleasure in walking, Father was only too glad to give me plenty of small pastoral duties, asking me to make visits that often took me to quite remote parts of the parish. My main delight, however, came from the sheer sensuous enjoyment of all the country sights, sounds and smells. Perhaps these, more than anything, lifted my spirits and made me feel better in body and mind.

My destination was usually one or other far-off cottage, where a family from Father's flock would be eking out a precarious existence. Invariably they seemed delighted to have a visitor and I'd be profusely welcomed, then given a lavish tea with scones or oatcakes spread, if I was lucky, with fresh butter and jam.

Being hungry from my long walk I always ate heartily, which would please my hostess. To begin with we would chat agreeably about the weather and the prospect of a good or bad harvest. Surprisingly often the conversation would then turn to more serious and momentous matters of the day – even political affairs such as Gladstone's struggles to solve the Irish question and the implications of land reform generally for Scottish tenant farmers. Matters like that were seldom if ever discussed at the manse and later I thought it strange that Will in particular showed little or no interest in politics.

But no one, either at home or on my parish visits, ever talked about better education for girls or discussed women's right to vote as we do nowadays. That would have been a step too far in those far-off times. Instead, I would be invited to have a good look at the family's cattle and garden before being accompanied a mile or so down the road on my journey home.

* * * *

If my parents had both passed on to me a love of plants and flowers, it was Will who yet further stimulated my interest in the stars and planets – after Father had first introduced us to astronomy with his magic lantern slides. On clear, frosty nights Will would point out and name all the constellations until I could identify them unaided. It was an interest I shared with Charlie, who went on to become professor of astronomy at Madras. In autumn, we looked out for meteor showers and saw particularly brilliant displays of the Leonids. The manse possessed a wonderful atlas of star maps but it eventually disappeared – probably when Charlie went off to University.

Charlie's middle name was Michie, from the maiden name of my Granny on Father's side of the family. Though four years older than me, he was a perfect playmate in my younger days and his practical skills were called upon whenever we needed something repaired or constructed for our games. In his teens he and the boarding boys had built a fine, solid workshop in a secluded corner of the garden. Complete with gothic windows rescued from the church when new ones were installed, it had a large workbench and a huge assortment of tools on which Charlie spent all his pocket money. The workshop was his own special province but he welcomed visits from me whenever I was bored with womanly activities in the manse. Father disapproved of Charlie's practical aptitude and did nothing to encourage it. That seemed very odd to me in view of his own apprenticeship as wood-turner but I imagine he felt that manual skills were in some way an inferior talent.

Like the older boys, Charlie was taught at home by Father until he went to University but, while highly talented at Maths just as his older brothers were, his intense dislike of Latin and Greek was an affront to Father and at times distinctly strained the relationship between father and son so that I think Charlie was pleased to leave home for King's College. By that time Will was in his post at the Free

Church College and the two lived together very amicably in Aberdeen. To everyone's surprise, Charlie gained a prize at King's for Latin verse, an achievement which did much to restore him to Father's good graces.

I have written already about our personal gardens, inspected almost every day by Father and Mother on their evening perambulations. I lavished most care and attention though on that patch of virgin soil out of which Lucy and I had painstakingly created a secret garden of our own at the edge of the woods beyond the garden dyke – until the cows sealed its fate. This was a spot which my parents didn't ever visit and in a curious fashion it was therefore something special and very personal to me.

Lucy enjoyed gardening well enough but her greatest love was extended towards all the animals. Looking after the hens and chickens was her special responsibility and she would engage in long chats with them, mimicking their crowing and clucking so cleverly that we teasingly called her our "laughing kookaburra". Then there were all the rabbits and the miscellany of wild creatures that we collected intermittently over the childhood years. She maintained that love for years and much later, when living in India with Charlie, she prided herself on giving individual names to all the poultry in the very large brood she kept there. And while staying in the heart of Aberdeen with Bella, Lucy established her own chicken run and cared for each bird in a quite touching way, going from one to the other with water or grain and speaking personally to each. I am sure that caring attitude was reflected in her later devotion to nursing. Though very different in our personalities, Lucy and I loved each other dearly and seldom if ever fell out.

Even more than our secret garden, it was my butterfly

collection that became the grand passion of my teenage days at the manse. The first stirrings of interest came, I think, during that summer after we had all returned from Edinburgh – Will to prepare for his professional work at Aberdeen Free Church College and I to readjust painfully to living far out in the country, away from all the stimulus and social intercourse of city life.

Will wrote home from Aberdeen, mentioning that the younger brother of a friend of his was in poor health and needed a strengthening dose of country life. The boy's mother was widowed and so payment was out of the question but as always my parents responded with a generous invitation to this youngster, Peter by name, that he should come to stay at Keig for as long as he wished.

Lucy and I looked forward to a new playmate but Peter proved to be a lad of fourteen who thought himself above mixing with two girls younger than himself. Moreover, he had come from a large school in the city and I had the impression from the first encounter that his attitude towards us was condescending and more than slightly patronising.

We girls took offence at this but I showed my resentment more openly than Lucy – it was with some justice that folk always said, "Yon lassie Alice has a richt guid conceit o hersel". Not only did I regard myself as well-educated – hadn't I been at school in the capital? – but I was more conscious than Lucy of my dignity and status as a daughter of the manse.

So my initial feelings towards Peter were hostile. Until, that is, I was privileged to see his butterfly colletion for the first time – when immediately I became enthralled. It wasn't that Peter himself pursued his hobby with any special passion (I think he was already growing out of it) but he had brought his butterfly net with him and very willingly paraded his skill at catching the insects. At first I thought it quite impossible to emulate him and I wasn't willing to let him see how clumsy I was. So I decided to learn all by myself.

One bright day in early autumn I happened to find myself all alone in the garden after the midday meal. A shimmering butterfly came winging past and settled with folded wings on one of the shrubs: it turned out to be a Red Admiral but at the time I had no idea of the different butterfly names or species. I later discovered they were rare in our part of the country: indeed I never found a Red Admiral at Keig again. Awkwardly I tried to catch it in my cupped hands but it flew off at once and went out of sight.

My parents had just come out to enjoy the afternoon sunshine and I ran breathlessly to them. "You'll never guess what I've seen – the most gorgeous butterfly you could imagine. He was on that bush there, just inches away. But he's gone now."

"No, he hasn't," said Mother. "See, there he is, over by the gentians."

This was a glorious patch of blue in a flowerbed that we had originally planted in memory of Mary Jane and which I still carefully tended.

"May I?"

Both parents nodded in assent and at my second go I managed to catch the Red Admiral without hurting it in any way. And that was the start of a hobby which for a time became almost an obsession. First there was the gruesome business of placing the butterfly in my killing bottle of laurel leaves. Then I had to make a display case – the grocer, I believe, gave me a low, glass-covered box, large enough at first for my collection. I lined it with stiff white paper and then cut triangular pieces of card as a backing for the wings which were carefully pinned on to tiny circles of cork, cut neatly from a bottle stopper.

My fascination with butterflies grew apace and I would regularly set off, equipped with my butterfly net and matchboxes for specimens, skirting the woods, fields and riverbank. Walking by the banks of the Don was strictly forbidden by the Laird but that made the act all the more pleasurable.

So far, so good; but I still knew nothing at all about butterflies and it wasn't until Will came back home the following summer bringing me a fine reference book on Lepidoptera that I could begin to take things seriously. Now I could begin to understand the Linnaean system of classification into families, genera and species, and start to learn the art of identification from wing colour and body shape. Gradually I could grasp the difference for example between butterflies (*Rhepalocera*) with a thickening at the end of their antennae, and moths (*Heterocera*) with their tapered and often feathery antennae. Difficult though all the technical words were, I found them easier than geological terms, perhaps because I was so fascinated by the subject.

Then Will bought me a second book that dealt with all the technicalities of collection and display, but it recommended using only the very best equipment which had to be bought at great expense from a specialist shop down in London. That was far away beyond my means but at least I now knew what was wanted and our local joiner, whose workshop was down by the Don and who had been a very good friend to Charlie, soon knocked up suitable boards from soft wood into which the pins could be easily inserted. These were every bit as good as the cork linings of expensively manufactured display boxes.

Killing the insects was a problem. The leaves of Spanish laurel from the garden were quite lethal enough to deal with the smaller butterflies and moths but larger species could take hours or days to die. That was an unpleasant experience for me even in those far-off days when everyone was so familiar with both human and animal death. I tried using ether, remarkably easy to obtain from the chemist, but even that was unsatisfactory for dealing with the bigger insects which had to be softened in mercuric chloride for a week or so before being mounted.

At first Lucy and Bertie joined in with me enthusiastically. We each had our own butterfly nets and would set off together on hunting expeditions. For them the novelty soon wore off, however, and I was left to pursue my great passion all alone, which suited me very well.

Once people began to hear of my collection or saw me out and about on my collecting sprees, they would bring me specimens, almost always dead and not always well preserved. In turn, visitors to the manse would regularly be honoured with the opportunity of admiring my growing collection. Housing the specimens became a real problem once the collection outgrew my original case. By now anyway I wanted to show off my collection systematically and so I needed a whole set of boxes, though I knew I could never aspire to a proper display cabinet.

Mother as usual came up with the answer after one of her visits to Aberdeen. She went regularly to the city with Father twice a year and while he attended the Church Synod she would go off to buy dressmaking material from one of the large clothing shops. One day she spotted a neat pile of flat boxes on the counter, of the kind used for holding men's shirts. The shopkeeper readily gave her one to bring home for me and after that she never failed to come home with one or two more of these, all of which were identical and so admirably suited to being converted into matching containers for my collection.

In each instance I first reinforced the lid by glueing cord all round, then lined the box with cork strips, carefully glued into place. Next I wrote out in my best copperplate a label for each specimen, giving both the Latin and common names, so far as I could find these out, and finally added my own catalogue reference number, together with a note of the date and time of capture. That all sounds easy and straightforward but you must realise that to begin with I made lots of mistakes in identification and classification, which meant I had to constantly renew the labels and rearrange my specimens, a delicate and time-consuming task.

Serious collecting only began in the summer of the year after I had seen and caught my first Red Admiral: then the fascination of my new hobby really caught hold of me. By far the best territory for hunting was at the foot of Cairn William, not far from the manse, in a small, sunlit boggy strip of ground where the butterflies feasted greedily on thistles and other wild flowers. Behind stood a large stony outcrop where abundant cowslips and willow herb attracted them even more so. In early summer, as soon as lessons were over, I would race there across the heather and remain until Father's loud coo-ees called me home for dinner.

In 1875, Will invited his German friend, Dr Klein, by then Professor of Mathematics at Erlangen, for a walking holiday in the Scottish Highlands and the two of them stayed with us for several days. We offered Dr Klein our best oatcakes but he disliked them, later chewing a heather twig and remarking that it tasted better than oatcake. He examined my butterfly collection with great interest, noting that I had no examples of the Sphinx (hawk moth) family and recommending I should hunt for them in the willow trees – where sure enough I discovered two fat caterpillars that soon turned into chrysalids and emerged next summer as a fine pair.

Once someone came to say that an unusually large

butterfly was somewhere down by the joiner's workshop at the river. Everyone hunted for it and finally I was handed the very biggest of the Sphinx family – a Death's Head moth with its dark, yellow-streaked wings. I came across no more until visiting Frankfurt-on-Main with Lucy the following year, when another Death's Head moth flew in at our window, attracted by the light. Coincidentally, that visit happened at the same time as the retirement of the shopkeeper who had for years supplied Mother with my display boxes. My interest in collecting actively was diminishing anyway by then, for many new interests were coming into my life. It was time for me to emerge from my own chrysalis.

Decades later, when I was long since married and living in Germany, I was forced to give away my entire collection because of lack of space at home. That was quite distressing for me because so many poignant yet happy memories of life at the Manse of Keig were intimately bound up with it. Yet my treasures found a suitable home in my daughter Jeannie's school in Aachen.

PART TWO

LATER DAYS

After Will had taken up his new post at Aberdeen in November, 1870, life at the manse of Keig continued relatively peacefully for the next five years. He regularly visited us by train and wrote conscientiously whenever he went abroad, usually enclosing a batch of personal letters for each of us. I still cherish the very first letter he sent me after returning from Germany in 1871, the envelope elaborately inscribed:

Private   Privatissimum

Miss A. Smith

Private – for Alice only

But the contents would seem very innocuous today. I had asked him to tell me everything about how the German country folk dressed and so he duly gave me an elaborate description, complete with little illustrations, of the men's smocks and the women's print dresses – ". . . short enough to show their white stockings and bright garters. The dress is square and low in front showing a thick white chemise high at the neck. The hair gathered up into a high knot at the head – dragged back from the face and ears and topped by a little black silk cap or rather cushion: N.B. not a chignon but a top knot, the hair on all sides pulled up to the top."

And there was much more in the same vein, all demonstrating Will's care over the smallest detail, even when writing to a thirteen year old. You can imagine how proud I was to get such personal letters. In those

Victorian days, it was considered more than a little improper for a man even to refer to such an intimate article of clothing as a chemise. A year or so later, when Will had begun to learn Arabic, he told me how the word was mistakenly believed to have come from that language but that his scholarly friends would look disapprovingly at him when he mentioned the fact.

Will's love for Germany had begun with his visit there in 1867, when he stayed in Bonn. That was the first of many more, the second being in 1869 in the company of John Sutherland Black, a fellow-student from New College who was to become my brother's closest friend and in later days his colleague at the Encyclopaedia Britannica offices in Edinburgh. At Professor Tait's request, Will had promised to visit as many as possible of the scientific laboratories for which the German universities in those days were famous, in order to pick up "wrinkles" for the new physics laboratory that Tait was meaning to set up with my brother's help at Edinburgh University.

So he was kept very busy indeed, going around with letters of introduction to all the most eminent German physicists of the day while at the same time listening spellbound to Albrecht Ritschl's lectures in theology – very advanced by Scottish standards in those days yet less extreme than those of the "notorious" Tübingen school.

Two years later, however, Will took Nellie with him on his summer trip to Germany and I have told you already about the unhappy consequences of her love affair there. That had worried Will deeply – but my own appetite for travel had grown still greater and I began to hint broadly that it was now *my* turn to go abroad with him. After all, hadn't I followed Nellie in going to Edinburgh? And hadn't that been an important step in my growing up? And wasn't I now at eighteen a very sensible young lady? So, at the end of the university term in 1876, he gave in.

"Alice," he said to me, quite out of the blue one morning, "George Reid and I are meaning to make a tour of the Continent this spring. Black and I wanted to do that back in 1870 but the war stopped us then. How would you and Lucy both like to come part of the way with us? We couldn't take you the whole tour but I'll find somewhere decent for the pair of you to stay for a few months or so in a nice German town, where you can really get to grips with the language. And I'll arrange classes for you both in music and drawing too."

Well, that seemed absolutely perfect: drawing lessons *and* foreign travel! As usual, my eldest brother had turned up trumps and I realised that he must have used all his powers of persuasion to convince our parents that we would be quite safe. He did find some difficulty though in tracking down a suitable place for Lucy and me to live in Germany but eventually learned of a minister's widow who was willing to accommodate us in Frankfurt-on-Main.

Now, during their tour, Will and George Reid busily kept a detailed log of their journey: they called it *Notes and Sketches* and made elaborate plans beforehand to have it privately printed the moment they arrived home. Will did most of the writing while George drew all the illustrations. When given a copy later, I was quite put out to discover there was not the slightest mention of Lucy and me accompanying them, apart from a single sentence noting that the two travellers had been able to see very little of Frankfurt because (so Will had written), "G.R. had to nurse his cold and W.R.S. to look after his sisters and establish them in Eschenheimer Landstrasse beyond the Eschenheimer Thor."

The four of us had set off in high spirits in mid-April, by

way of London, Antwerp, Bruges, Ghent, Aachen and Cologne, seeing all the sights, visiting every famous museum, church and art gallery on the way and also experiencing for the first time the thrill of dining – and even wining! – in restaurants, a very adult experience indeed for us girls. In many ways, my brother seemed quite different from the generally serious young man I had known in Keig and Edinburgh. He was far more relaxed and light-hearted, interested in everything we saw or did in our travels, and quite unconscious of the problems that would face him on his return home.

The weather at the end of April was marvellous and the trees everywhere were just coming into leaf so that the scenery was absolutely beautiful. Finally, after taking a steamer up the Rhine as far as Rüdesheim, we all went on by train to Frankfurt, arriving there just as it grew dark. Will then introduced us to "Frau Pastor", our landlady, who solemnly promised to take every possible care of us once he and George had departed. But the reality was to prove very different. Lucy and I were immediately left entirely on our own and though we bravely went around, dictionaries in hand, trying to engage in conversation, no one took the slightest heed of our attempts. It turned out the "Frau Pastor" was totally preoccupied with her daughter's imminent wedding and even went off to visit relatives, abandoning us to the care of a very dull-witted maid, the kind of girl we would have described at home in Aberdeenshire as a "fushionless quine" who didn't even provide us with decent food to eat at mealtimes.

This was hardly turning out to be the pleasurable adventure we had expected. Day after day we both grew increasingly miserable, yet there seemed no escape and no white knight to rescue us. We didn't know Will's exact travel plans and he'd left us no forwarding address. Poor

Lucy, who had never been far from home before, felt even more unhappy than I did and pleaded with me to write home. I knew though that telling our parents about the plight we were in would make them simply frantic with worry.

After some weeks had passed in this way, it was Lucy herself who came up with the answer. "Look, Alice," she said, "aren't Father and Mother due to go off to the General Assembly in Edinburgh for a whole week. We can write to Nellie without Mamma or Papa knowing anything about it. And she may know how to get in touch with Will."

That indeed did the trick. By chance, Will was at Keig when Nellie got our letter and so it was he of course who miraculously turned up to save us. During our time with "Frau Pastor", our one mainstay and comfort in Frankfurt had been our drawing-master, Herr Junkers, who had at once spotted our unhappiness and had asked his wife to invite us regularly for meals and excursions. And when Will arrived on the scene Frau Junkers suggested we should go to live with her old aunt, Frau Brisbois, who had long been used to looking after paying guests. The new arrangement worked out perfectly and from then on we were really treated as if we had been members of the family, besides being given every opportunity and encouragement to talk German. So we went on with our studies and were now able to enjoy them to the full.

A few weeks later, one of our weekly letters from Keig gave us the startling information that Nellie was about to be engaged. And, still more surprising, her fiancé was to be none other than the man appointed as Father's assistant, James Hamilton Allan. My first reaction was of delight that Nellie had at last overcome her mad and fruitless infatuation with Gerhard and that one of us at long last was to be married. Then, much to my annoyance, I realised that we couldn't possibly be present at the wedding, which was to take place in less than a month. Couldn't they possibly have waited? It seemed almost indecent haste to me.

But Lucy seemed to share none of my feelings and her behaviour puzzled me greatly. She was neither elated by the news nor indignant, like me, at the fact we wouldn't be present. Instead, she became uncharacteristically pale and downcast, in complete contrast to her usual happy-go-lucky temperament. She mooned around interminably and barely spoke for hours at a time. Though that behaviour wore off in due course, I only learned the truth more than a year later, after Nellie's marriage had taken place and we were both back home at Keig. One evening we were lying in bed, for we still slept together in the old nursery at the manse, when Lucy blew out the candle and then spoke very quietly to me.

"I've never told you this before, Alice, and nobody else in the family knows, but that man Hamilton, our brother-in-law, asked me to marry him before you and I went off to Germany. It happened right here in the garden, down in Bachelor's Corner. He actually went down on one knee and proposed! It was all very romantic and heart-stopping at the time, I must say, and as you can guess I was bowled over with excitement. He'd never been all that attentive to me before – certainly never held my hand or even tried to kiss me.

"He said something like this to me, very stiffly, in his usual earnest fashion: 'My dear Miss Smith' – and Lucy mimicked him beautifully, as only she could – 'I have admired you ever since coming here to work with your Papa, and I believe you would make a truly admirable helpmeet for me. I realise you are still very young and that you will soon be going off to Germany for quite a lengthy stay, but I ask you to think carefully about my proposal of marriage while you are gone. If you feel suitably inclined to marry me, we can then ask your Mamma and Papa for their approval and blessing as soon as you return home.'"

"Did you really take him seriously?" I asked.

"Of course. Why ever shouldn't I? I was absolutely bowled over. Here was I, the youngest of us all, going to be the first girl in the family to be married. It was an absolute dream come true. Wouldn't you have felt the same?"

I sat upright, my heart thumping. "Well, I don't know. How did you answer him?"

"I didn't know what to say at first. Naturally I blushed scarlet and for quite a few minutes said nothing at all. But I know I was trembling. The fact that you and I were going away to Germany meant the dream wouldn't turn into reality for quite a long while, which I suppose was quite a comfort in some ways. And he still hadn't touched me at all – not even held my hand. But of course I thanked him very politely, said how honoured I was etc., etc., and that I hoped I would be able to live up to his expectations. That was as much as to say I accepted. So now you can understand how that letter from home came as such a terrible shock to me. It was quite horrible and devastating. He hadn't even ditched me for some girl I didn't know. He'd simply switched his attentions to Nellie as soon as I was out of sight. So handy for him. He didn't have to look beyond the garden gate for another choice of wife."

And she began to weep bitterly while I put my arms around her and cried too. I don't believe she ever told anyone else about Hamilton's betrayal. Poor, poor Lucy! Poor Nellie too – the marriage was not to turn out a happy one. They were married at Strathdon in 1876 where her husband had been called to his first parish but they stayed there only a few years before moving to Sellafirth on the island of Yell in Shetland. James Hamilton turned out to be a weak, shiftless character, unsuited really to being a minister, and quite lacking any of Nellie's drive and initiative. They had no children and it was Nellie who ended up doing the lion's share of the pastoral work amongst the congregation there, holding classes for the children and becoming greatly admired by the local folk. She would even go up into the pulpit when Hamilton was unfit to do so.

Life up there in the far north was very hard for everyone. Conditions were primitive and people had a struggle simply to survive. Husbands were often lost at sea, leaving their widows to bring up a large family unsupported. But they managed somehow, mainly by knitting those wonderful shawls that Queen Victoria so admired.

Her husband died in 1897 but Nellie stayed on there for another thirteen years before moving to live closer to Aberdeen, buying a smart villa called Lochnagar at Peterculter. When she died of flu in 1917, a Shetland obituary said of her: "She would have graced the most select society in the land, but she elected to live and labour here, giving of her best for the good of all." My sister Lucy, on the other hand, was destined to remain unmarried throughout her life.

* * * *

As for me, it was in Frankfurt that I met my future husband, Hans Thiele. His stepmother, Gertrude, was the daughter of our kindly landlady, Frau Brisbois. The family were Huguenot in origin and therefore eminently appropriate from my parents' point of view. Hans had just finished an ironmonger's apprenticeship and was ambitious to set up his own business. In 1876 he was on the lookout for a suitable opening in the Frankfurt area but that was to take some time. Neither of us yet spoke the other's language very well and so our relationship developed in a very natural and ordinary way through a mutual wish to help each other learn. Hans started to seek out my company more and more often, till I became aware that on both sides deeper feelings of attachment were growing steadily. My favourite hobby by then was art, thanks to the tuition from Herr Junkers, and Hans greatly liked my little watercolour landscapes and flower paintings.

I longed to share my feelings with Lucy but she was always so withdrawn and dour in those days at Frankfurt. Nor dared I write home about the blossoming romance, fearful of getting a very negative reaction from my parents after Nellie's unlucky German love affair. Yet keeping it all to myself made me feel deeply guilty, for it had been thoroughly instilled in us that "secrets" were wrong – a form of disobedience in fact. Yet I should so much have liked to have someone to tell me at this stage how I ought to behave. I spent many a sleepless night before making up my mind to take the risk and confess in a letter home that Hans and I were thinking about becoming engaged.

As you can imagine, the news was not at all welcome at first but Mother wrote to Frau Brisbois who reassured her that I was in no danger and that Hans was a "very respectable young fellow". And Will, who knew the family well by now, was fortunately on my side. However, after a year in Germany Lucy and I were called back home: "You two girls have been long enough away from us all," Father wrote, " and there is now a real threat of war in the Balkans."

Both Father and Mother agreed to travel across to Germany to meet the family and then to escort us home. They expressed themselves satisfied with my intended husband, Hans, and to my pleasure I was allowed to stay some time longer. Yet once our formal engagement was pronounced in September, 1877, I had finally to leave for home. Lucy and our parents had in fact gone already to visit relatives in London.

Of course it was good to be back amongst all our familiar surroundings but an unspoken question hung in the air. What was I to do? Lucy was only eighteen but I was now twenty and I could hardly spend my time as a lady of leisure. There was no alternative other than to look for a post as governess somewhere and Will as ever soon found a suitable family. I was to go at once to Aberdeen to give lessons to the young children of one of his closest friends in the city, Dr John Forbes White, a well-known art collector and man of the world.

I had a flair for working with children and greatly enjoyed teaching the White family but at the same time found myself at a low ebb both physically and emotionally. Most of all, I missed Hans' company and so sat late into the night writing long and ardent letters to him; in turn, all that lack of exercise made my back trouble flare up again so that I couldn't sleep a wink and spent hours wandering restlessly around in Will's house in Aberdeen where I was living. He was away at the time – down in London working very happily on the Revision of the Old Testament – and I grew intensely nervous, worrying unreasonably at nights over the slightest unusual noise outside in the street.

During the day, Will's housekeeper, Jane, did her best to help but was ultimately at a loss to know what to do for me and it was only after a most unexpected visit from home-loving Bella, whose present of a cake she'd baked specially caused me to break down in a flood of tears, that Mother was alerted to my condition and insisted I go to see Dr Davidson, an Aberdeen physician whom we'd known ever since George and Will were students. He gave orders that I should immediately return home for, he said, "You have far too delicate a constitution for teaching." Instead I was to rest for prolonged periods on my back.

Back at home, Mother had our friendly local carpenter make me a long wooden board which was propped at an angle to make an inclined plane facing the old nursery window. So I was reduced to lying there, hour after hour, staring out impotently towards my beloved garden. Things grew still worse: another doctor then had me encased in a plaster cast for five months and I had to be moved downstairs since I could no longer negotiate the stairs.

So the final years of 1870s dragged by most miserably for me, while the rest of the family were far more preoccupied with those momentous events associated with Will's fateful trial for heresy at the hands of the Free Church Assembly. Moments of triumph in that bitter and long-drawn-out conflict were mixed with long weeks of despair and even Will, whose mental and physical resilience in the face of such adversity seemed inexhaustible, began to show signs of strain and talked eventually of throwing the whole business up. He might even go to Glasgow, he said, where there was a vacant chair of mathematics at the university.

I was buoyed up briefly by a visit to Keig from Hans. Beforehand, I worried excessively about the outcome of our meeting. Nellie's experience with Gerhard had by no means been forgotten and I could well imagine that the whole family were apprehensive. However, Hans acquitted himself well and his behaviour met with not the slightest criticism from anyone at the manse. Father and Mother seemed even more impressed with him than at the time of their original meeting in Frankfurt. Though a Lutheran, he was wholly sympathetic towards our Scottish Presbyterianism and happily attended all the church services as well as participating in daily family worship. So, by the end of his visit, our joint future seemed set fair. What I

could not then know was just how long the engagement was
to be. Hans was determined to wait until he had successfully
established his own business and that was not to happen
until the end of 1882 when, with financial help from Will, he
opened a shop in Bernburg on the river Saale.

Our wedding eventually took place in January, 1883, the
ceremony being held, as was common in those days, in the
family home at Skene Place, Aberdeen, to which we had
moved after Father's retirement two years previously. Will
was one of the two witnesses and, rather to my surprise, he
had taken the precaution of having a marriage contract
drawn up in German to ensure that my rights would be
safeguarded in the event of my husband's death. The whole
occasion was both joyous yet solemn, because everyone was
all too conscious that I would now be leaving my
Aberdeenshire roots for good. I felt natural pride in my
wedded status but was also more than a little scared of
becoming a married woman and living so far from the
family to whom I had always looked for guidance and
support. Even Mother lost her customary stoicism and we
wept in each other's arms when the final parting came.

* * * *

Now I must begin to draw my story to a close and give you a
brief sketch of the family's varied fortunes after the mile-
stone of my marriage. Bertie, our youngest brother, was
twenty-one by 1883. Always an amicable yet delicate,
nervous boy, he had great difficulty learning his letters and I
have told you about the painful scenes which so often took
place in the schoolroom when Father tried to teach him the
rudiments of Latin. I can no longer remember when Father
finally realised the futility of the daily confrontation and
abandoned the struggle. Bertie was a shy, very self-

absorbed lad, seldom taking any part in our games and having no real interest in the garden. His one great passion was stamp-collecting and Will, who was now corresponding with scholars throughout Europe and beyond, used to send him all kinds of interesting foreign stamps. After 1882, when Will moved back to Edinburgh to work there on the Encyclopaedia Britannica, Bertie joined him and they shared a small flat in the heart of the city.

By 1885, when Hans and I came to Scotland for a short holiday, I found to my delight that Bertie had obtained a job working in an Aberdeen bank. Out of his own earnings he gave my first child, little Jeannie, a most beautiful teething coral and presented me also with a Latin New Testament that I'd longed to possess. However, his failing health soon forced him to give up working and it was eventually discovered that he was suffering from very advanced tuberculosis. I was fortunate to see him once more, on a second visit to Aberdeen in 1887. My joy at being back with the family was sadly marred by the realisation that Bertie was now beyond recovery. He could tolerate no noise at all and for that reason I went to stay in a small flat nearby so that Mother could nurse him constantly at home. He died peacefully in December of that year.

After her return from Germany, Lucy began studying with a new determination under Father's tuition. In 1879 a close friend of Will, John F. Maclennan, had asked if Lucy might go to Algiers to act as governess for his step-daughter, Ella. Like so many more in those days, Ella's father was desperately ill with tuberculosis. At the last moment it was decided that Davos in Switzerland would be more therapeutic and Lucy accordingly accompanied the family there. Ella was proving to be quite a difficult child and needed careful management. The family returned home to a house in Kent where Mr Maclennan died in 1881. Lucy remained with his widow, acting as governess at first to Ella and then as companion to her mother until Mrs Maclennan's death some years later.

The skills and experience she had by then acquired enabled her to become a nurse at St Thomas's Hospital in London where she rose eventually to be assistant matron. The work was hard and the hours very long, yet Lucy thoroughly enjoyed doing the kind of work for which her cheerful, active personality was ideal. Around about the year 1909, Lucy picked up a hospital infection which quickly developed into pneumonia and we feared for the worst as she lay gravely ill. Still, she had a tough, wiry constitution and recovered in due course, coming back to recuperate in Aberdeen. Meantime Charlie had repeatedly urged Lucy to join him out in India and this she eventually did, remaining there until her death in 1922.

I seem to have told you little so far about our brother, Charlie, apart from mentioning his practical ability and woodworking skills. He was almost four years older than me and for that reason closer in terms of companionship to Nellie. Indeed, the two had a very close bond in childhood. Like the older boys, Charlie was taught at home by Father who approved of his flair for maths but was never slow to show his disappointment that Charles had little aptitude for learning the classical languages. Schoolroom sessions were accordingly often stormy, though nothing like so upsetting to the rest of us as those between Father and Bertie.

Will's appointment to the Hebrew chair at the Free Church College in 1870 had coincided with Charlie's entry to King's College in Aberdeen and so it was ideal that the two should share Will's rented flat there. After graduating, Charlie went off to Edinburgh to continue his scientific studies there and then found employment with a large firm in London which was manufacturing submarine cables for the telegraphic links that were rapidly being established world-wide. I can't be sure, but it's possible that Professor Tait and Sir William Thomson, Will's old friends, were responsible for putting Charles' name forward to the company. Both men had been much involved in the technical aspects of submarine telegraphy and Thomson (later Lord Kelvin) had been instrumental in solving the many teething problems of the first transatlantic cable in 1858.

One summer's day in 1875 a letter arrived at the manse from Charlie, announcing that he must leave in one week's time for the West Indies to begin laying underwater cables between the Caribbean islands. It was, he explained, "a first-rate opportunity" but he was most disappointed at being unable to come home and say farewell to all the family. That was equally hard for the rest of us because we couldn't imagine one of our family being so far from us, and not knowing when he might return. Worse still, both parents were away at the time. We all put our heads together and debated what could be done.

Bella said, "Why don't we get a photograph taken to send him as a parting gift?" And so we all trooped off to nearby Alford where the local photographer duly took a group picture of the four of us girls along with Bertie. But we couldn't afford to have more than one copy made and no trace of it survives.

Charlie did return home, however, a few months later. There had been a sudden loss of confidence in the telegraph industry and jobs were scarce. Unable to find work immediately, he went back to Edinburgh, where I remember visiting him briefly in 1876 on our way to Germany with Will and George Reid. Quite soon, however, Charlie was fortunate enough to be appointed to the post of professor of mathematics and physics at Madras Christian College and for a second time he set off abroad, this time to make a permanent home overseas. His departure was especially hard for all of us since it came at the start of Will's long battle with the Free Church. The two brothers corresponded regularly of course but Charlie could be of no direct help.

Life in India appeared to suit him eminently and he pursued a successful teaching career at Madras while also following his special interests in meteorology and astronomy. He soon struck up a close friendship with the director of the local observatory, Norman Robert Pogson, who was in poor health and therefore valued all the more my brother's assistance. On the director's death in 1893, Charlie was asked to take over the post, which entailed being chief astronomer for the region within the Indian Civil Service. A new observatory was in the process of being established in the Palani Hills at Kodaikanal, some two hundred miles south-west of Madras, and Charlie then moved to that spot where he was to remain for the rest of his life, taking an active part in the actual building work, pursuing research and contributing regularly to scientific journals.

In 1883 there had occurred that tremendous natural event, the volcanic eruption on the island of Krakatoa in Indonesia, with incredible meteorological phenomena that were to persist for many months. People throughout the world were fascinated and puzzled by the climate changes and the strangely coloured sunlight, which we now know were the result of a volcanic explosion quite unprecedented in its magnitude. Charlie of course took part in the great debate although the views he published then were later regarded as wrong. Without modern knowledge about wind speeds high in the upper atmosphere, he concluded that the effects produced by the massive dust cloud could not possibly have reached Madras as quickly as they did.

Being located in the hill country, Kodaikanal was pleasantly cool and certainly a healthier place in which to live than the crowded, oppressive environment of Madras. So Charlie seldom took advantage of the generous home leave to which all senior government officials were entitled and I recall him taking only one proper holiday back in Scotland, during 1909, after Lucy's illness, when all five of us (Charlie, Nellie, Bella, Lucy and myself) took a cottage near Alford and were able to return together to the favourite haunts of our childhood. That was a wonderful time. The sight of Bennachie and Cairn William, the sharp, resinous scent of the pine trees, the spring of the heather beneath our feet – even the squelch of mud as we trekked through the marshland beside the Don – all those sights and sounds poignantly evoked the childhood years spent many years ago at Keig. We parted with a firm resolution to meet again in six years' time but that year, 1914, saw the outbreak of the Great War and put an end to long-distance travel.

Just before our meeting, as I have said, Lucy had given in to Charlie's repeated request that she should come to India and live with him. Now well into middle age, Lucy had long abandoned thoughts of marriage and the prospect of a peaceful retirement in the Indian hills must have held considerable appeal for her. Charlie had a beautiful home and garden beside the Kodaikanal observatory. There were domestic animals too in plenty for Lucy to care for and talk to, just as she had done in the early days at Keig. Moreover, Charlie was about to attend a Royal Geographical Society conference in Australia and the chance of travelling to the other side of the world was an added attraction for her.

By the end of the war, however, Charlie was himself a sick man. He and our sister made the long journey back to

Scotland in the spring of 1919, meaning to stay, but Charlie could no longer stand the harsh climate nor, so he declared, the narrow Scottish mentality. With deep misgivings, Lucy returned to India with him, faced with having to nurse a brother whose mental and physical condition was steadily deteriorating. That took the last of Lucy's strength and by a cruel twist of fate she herself caught a tropical infection at the start of 1922 and died six months before our brother's own life came to an end.

My relationship with Bella was not always an easy one. More than eight years older than me, she could never be a natural playmate to the younger ones in the family, nor was she physically able to run about as the rest of us did. After Mary Jane's death, Bella felt her place was in the home and, as Mother grew older, she gradually took increasing charge of the domestic management, becoming adept at cooking, baking and jam-making, not to mention needlework. But her bossiness towards the younger children constantly irked me and that awful episode that I told you about before – when I laboriously made two dresses out of muslin for my beloved but ugly doll, only to have Bella immediately surpass all my efforts by speedily running up a far smarter outfit for Lucy's doll – was something that rankled with me for months, if not years.

Lucy was certainly Bella's favourite sister and it was Lucy she insisted on taking with her on the rare occasions when she spent a few days staying with friends in the neighbourhood – the Scotts for example, who had lodged our parents for the first few weeks after their move to Keig in 1845 – or the Mitchell family at Auchnagatt who had similarly been staunch supporters of the Free Kirk from the earliest days. But beyond that single visit to Mother's relatives in London, when she visited the Crystal Palace to see the Great Exhibition, Bella refused to travel far away from home. Father's suggestion that she should go to Germany with Will like the rest of us was immediately dismissed out of hand: "I'll bide here at the manse, thank you all the same," was her blunt response.

An otherwise efficient, practical and industrious woman, Bella had quite a bit of our Aunt Mattie in her character, or so I always felt. Long before Father retired in 1881, Bella had taken full charge of the household and effortlessly took over the running of our Aberdeen flat in Skene Place. And after Father's death, in the Fountainhall Road house which Will had bought, Bella naturally took care of Mother there until her death in 1899. Will had stipulated that the property was to be shared by his two unmarried sisters, Lucy and Bella; but Lucy, as you know went off to India to join Charlie, and so Bella remained alone in the house, a rather sad and lonely figure, eking out a frugal existence there until Charlie's death in 1922 brought her an unexpected windfall in the shape of her brother's quite considerable fortune.

I last saw Bella in 1925, when I came to Scotland with my two daughters, Jeannie and Lucy. Though she had no time for my three boys – "they're just right Germans through and through," she would say – Bella had a very soft spot for her two nieces and would happily spoil them, just as Aunt Mattie had done with her nieces all those years before. On that last occasion we spent another delightfully evocative holiday back at Keig, boarding there with our old manse postman and his wife. Even Bella, by then seventy-five, seemed rejuvenated.

Bella lived on to see her eighty-ninth year. Her final gesture, a fine one, was to bequeath to Aberdeen Art Gallery the paintings of our parents and of Will by George Reid and his brother Archibald. There they may still be seen.

Last of all, I must say a little more about Will himself. For Father, whose own education had been so long thwarted by poverty, Will's academic success was the fulfilment of all his personal longing for achievement and each honour gained by his son was a source of deep satisfaction. From an early age he treated Will as an intellectual equal and for the rest of their lives both were, I am sure, a continuing source of inspiration to one another. Will and his father could argue for ages without the older man showing the slightest sign of that irritability which became an increasing element of his character as the years passed.

For his part, Will very seldom lost patience with any of us younger children and I have mentioned how wholeheartedly he entered into all our games, becoming a child himself once more. I know that he was often much less forbearing with others and some of his letters home from New College describe how fiercely he crossed swords even then with those who could not accept his point of view. He was even sharply critical of those professors whose knowledge or lecturing skills fell below his expectations.

No one else I knew could work so hard and with such sustained concentration than my brother Will. Who else could have pursued their own studies so successfully while at the same time tutoring the junior Hebrew class *and* acting as Professor Tait's assistant in physics at the University? There is one story about his work there which he enjoyed telling us about in later times, after he had presented Bertie with a copy of Stevenson's *Treasure Island*.

"When I was working for Tait in Edinburgh," he said with a chuckle, " I had the particular duty of pointing out to his less promising students all their mathematical blunders. One of those students was the now quite famous author of this novel – Robert Louis Stevenson – and by his own account as well as mine he was the most idle of students, though sharp enough in his own way. Whenever I tried to correct his mistakes, Stevenson would unfailingly do his best to divert me from the task! For example, he'd say to me with his usual winning smile: 'Mr Smith, I confess I have never truly fathomed the true meaning of Christ's atonement. You are probably the only man in Scotland capable of explicating that formidable theological conundrum to me. I'd be mighty *obleeged* to you if you would do so.'

"Of course I knew his ploy and *he* knew that I knew it. But I doubt if any of the other students understood the game. *They* thought he was ragging me. Years later, we were both members of the Savile Club down in London and I daresay we laughed together about it. Stevenson always had a clever way with words, even though he has sadly wasted his talents by writing adventure stories. But I will say that *Treasure Island* is good."

"Did he ever mention you in one of his pieces?" I asked.

"Well, there's that *Smith of Aiberdeen* poem. About the Scotsman coming home from abroad and going to all the different kirks. How does it go again?

> *Preacher on preacher, kirk on kirk –*
> *This yin's a stot an' thon's a stirk –*
> *A bletherin' clan, no worth a preen,*
> *As bad as Smith of Aiberdeen!*

But you know, Stevenson is really poking fun at all those folk who criticise the Christian religion without understanding the first thing about it. Poor Stevenson! He has trouble himself understanding such matters."

I have told you too how thrilled I was when Will offered to take me to Edinburgh to stay with him and Nellie. Going to school there was the high point of my childhood, even though it was cut short so abruptly. Sometimes I felt in those days that my brother was inclined to be over-protective towards us – even a little dictatorial when he refused to let me have butter. But that was a kind of strictness he shared with Father and it stemmed, I am sure, from his often anxious sense of responsibility.

In 1870, the family and every one of his friends in Edinburgh hoped that Will would get the "Aberdeen thing", as he called it, and all were as delighted as Father when his appointment to the Hebrew chair was confirmed. Even Professor Tait was pleased, I think, for all that he and Sir William Thomson grumbled at what they called "this irretrievable loss to science". But for me his success had spelled the end of my school career.

In Aberdeen Will settled down for the next five peaceful years and in due course was able to buy himself a comfortable house in Crown Street. For a time, there was even a rumour that he had fallen in love with a girl he met socially, called Emma Yule. But fate stepped in when he was invited to contribute theological articles to the new edition of the Encyclopaedia Britannica. All young, up-and-coming experts in the different fields of knowledge saw it as a great honour and a fine opportunity to be asked to take part in that venture – and so did our brother. But only a few months after the first volumes of the Encyclopaedia came out at the very end of 1875, an unpleasant newspaper review in the *Edinburgh Courant* of Will's article "Bible" set the heather on fire (as Father put it). It was, the writer said, "an objectionable article" which had no business to be in a publication that would find its way into public libraries and private homes, where it might well corrupt the minds of the young – "Just like Socrates," Father commented bitterly. It was Will's conviction that the Bible must be read like any other book – critically and in its historical context – but the conservative opposition called that view "sheer German heresy".

Well, instead of fizzling out, the fire grew steadily stronger as the months and years passed, fanned by the dragon's breath of the so-called "Highland horde" that Father had once predicted would cause trouble to the Free Church. At first Will took the whole matter lightly and, as I've said, set off in high spirits on his European tour with George Reid, taking Lucy and me in tow. We girls could both testify that he seemed then not to have a care in the world.

As the pressure on him increased, however, he often became strained and anxious. First he voluntarily gave up his teaching duties until the matter should be finally settled; and by 1879 the outcome seemed so black that Will was seriously thinking of giving up the fight. Yet one year later, at the General Assembly in May, 1880, it appeared that he had won a remarkable victory against all the odds. Far from being convicted of heresy, Will was simply warned to be more guarded in the expression of his views. That of course was not the end. His next Encyclopaedia article (on "Hebrew Language and Literature") came out only six weeks later and with this fresh ammunition Will's enemies rallied to their cause again. Exactly one year later he was summarily dismissed from his post at Aberdeen, his teaching having being judged "unsettling" to his students. But it had been those self-same young men who presented Will with a fine mahogany grandfather clock which is still in my possession.

At home in Keig we had all followed the long-drawn-out affair, often with bated breath and always with considerable excitement. Most, though not all, of Father's congregation supported Will vigorously and there were constant messages of encouragement from all around the country – and from well beyond. Father himself never entertained the slightest doubt that his son Will was wholly in the right.

By 1881, I was twenty-three years old and took the news of Will's dismissal hard. To me it seemed the end of everything and I felt nothing but black despair. But events moved rapidly on and I was soon to be proved wrong, for Will now began work on the editorial side of the Encyclopaedia while continuing to provide a flood of articles from his own pen on theological and other topics. In addition, over the next two years he proceeded to give a series of Biblical lectures to huge audiences in Edinburgh and Glasgow. Those two sets of lectures were speedily published as soon as completed, the first entitled *The Old Testament in the Jewish Church*, the second *The Prophets of Israel*; and both became widely popular explanations of the "higher criticism" for which Will had been so harshly pilloried during the years before.

Two years later, he was offered the post of Lord Almoner's Reader in Arabic at Cambridge University and a completely new and highly congenial life opened up for him there. In 1887, he was appointed Librarian to the University and became a Fellow of Christ's College, which was to be his home to the end of his life. In 1887, Will's old teacher at Aberdeen University, Professor Bain, asked him to give a series of lectures there and it was out of those Burnett Lectures that there came Will's most famous book, *The Religion of the Semites*, still regarded as a pioneering work in the study of comparative religion. Both that book and *The Old Testament in the Jewish Church* were translated into German.

There were many painful events during those years: in particular, Bertie's death at the end of 1887 and then Father's passing away three years later after a long period of mental and physical decline. Only too soon after that, Will himself was overtaken by the fatal onset of the same tubercular condition which had already cost the lives of so many of my family: first Mary Jane, then George and Bertie. On the other hand, Will's great enterprise, the Encyclopaedia Britannica, was finally completed in 1888. As Chief Editor since 1883, he had steered it successfully to the end of its long voyage, having written hundreds of its articles, both great and small. In December, Will wrote to me how he had arranged a great celebratory dinner at Christ's College in honour of the event. Six months later, Will was appointed to the Thomas Adams Chair of Arabic at Cambridge.

Besides carrying out all those duties, he had never failed to care for us all. More than once he gave Hans and me a helping hand in the early days of our marriage, when we were beset by money problems or practical difficulties with the business. He took a warm interest naturally in our children, his nieces and nephews; and the three oldest never forgot his affection towards them.

My brother's personal journey through a turbulent but exciting life ended just over five years later. To my heartfelt grief, I was unable to travel over from Germany for the funeral but the letters from Nellie and Bella, along with the newspaper descriptions they sent me, were enough to bring the whole impressive scene vividly to life in my mind. After a short service in Christ's College, Cambridge, Will's body was brought by train to Aberdeen and on the following day, April 4, 1894, he was buried at home in Keig. I could picture it all so clearly: the little train on the branch line from Kintore to Alford, where once we had had so much fun secretly transferring our parents' silver wedding present; the arrival at Whitehouse station and the solemn, silent procession of black-suited men following the hearse bearing Will's coffin; the long two miles of narrow, winding country road to Keig village, past the Free Church and its manse, our old and beloved childhood home; and then the crossing of Telford's great stone archway over the Don to his final resting place within the kirkyard – ironically, that of the established church, where later two memorial tablets to my eldest brother and his father were unveiled.

Outside, you can see for yourselves the two fine granite headstones there, one for Will and the other for all the rest of the family buried at Keig. Will's epitaph, in Hebrew, is taken from the eleventh chapter of Isaiah:

And the spirit of the Lord shall rest upon him,
the spirit of wisdom and understanding,
the spirit of counsel and might,
the spirit of knowledge and of the fear of the Lord.

Back in Aberdeen, within King's College Chapel, Will's scholarship and piety are finely commemorated in the four stained-glass panels of one large window representing the Old Testament prophets Isaiah, Jeremiah, Ezekiel and Daniel. Below their portraits the Latin inscription reads:

With grief and admiration alike, his friends have dedicated this window to the memory of William Robertson Smith, L.L.D. of Aberdeen, Litt.D of Dublin, D.Th. of Strasburg, Professor at Cambridge; an alumnus of this university, greatly gifted, with a brilliant mind and outstanding in his scholarship. Born 1846; died 1894

16. Alice and Hans at the time of their marriage in 1883

17. The family in Aberdeen, Skene Place 1888 –
from the left: little Jeannie, Bella, Nellie, Mother, Father, Lucy and Alice

18. Bella, the housekeeper

19. Nellie, at last very ladylike

20. Charlie after his retirement

21. Lucy, the hospital matron

22. Will, in 1894 at Cambridge, by Sir George Reid

23. Alice and Hans in 1905   24. Alice in 1924

25. Golden Wedding in 1933 – Alice and Hans with all their children,
in-laws and grandchildren

FATHER'S STORY

By the time Lucy and I had reached adolescence, Father was well into his sixties and growing quite elderly. Apart from Bertie, he had no sons at home now and seemed to find increasing pleasure in the company of his daughters. Nellie was now abroad and Bella was wholly preoccupied with housekeeping so he began to spend more and more of his free time with his two youngest daughters. He had often told us tales of his early life and, somewhat to our surprise, proposed one day that Lucy and I should take turns taking down his life story from his dictation.

"It will give you practice with your handwriting," said he, quite forgetting that we were both now rather neat and skilful writers. We had no objection to the idea since it would help to pass the time during the long winter and also provide us, we hoped, with some amusement. I still have a copy of that memoir beside me and quite clearly remember also the conversation we had with Father as we went along. As it turned out, the story was never completed but stopped short at Father's graduation from King's College. Apart from inserting some of our whispered comments and the remarks Father made, I give his story below exactly as it was dictated.

"I was sent to school," began Father, "at a very early age. How early I cannot exactly say but my memory does not carry back to a time when I was unable to read. Probably my mother began to teach me as soon as I was able to speak plainly. The Bible seems to have been almost if not altogether the only lesson book made use of though I do recollect two elementary books in the house – but of these I remember only that the one had on its page the complot:

Let all the foreign tongues alone
Till you can read and spell your own

while the other contained long columns of words to be spelled and had, above its reading lessons, pictures of animals that were intended to illustrate the reading lessons and to impart to them a measure of interest."

Lucy had taken the first turn of writing and, looking over her shoulder, I saw she had written *complot* instead of *couplet* but knew Father would be irritated if I interrupted. So that mistake remains to this day.

"My first schoolmaster," he went on, "was a man by the name of William Selbie, a simple, loveable creature, with a kind word and a helping hand ready for everyone, young or old. He invariably wore long hose, knee breeches, a cutaway coat and a waistcoat that came down to his thighs. That waistcoat was remarkable for its two immense flapped pockets in front, in which were always to be found confections of sugared caraway seeds which he whimsically called *Justice Milleorum* and which he distributed for praiseworthy behaviour or for the comfort of little ones in distress.

"His school stood on the bank of the Justice Mill burn."

"So that's why he called the sweets *Justice Milleorum,*" laughed Lucy.

"Don't interrupt!" said Father. "Where was I? Ah, William Selbie's school. The school was set directly next to the lower meal mill of that name. It had the appearance of a long shed and had seemingly been built as a weaving shop capable of holding ten or twelve looms. There was a row of small windows on each side and the floor was of earth. When turned into a schoolroom, its one door was made to open upon a narrow passageway from front to back which divided the area into two unequal parts, the larger given over to school work, the smaller for the master's dwelling-house.

"William Selbie's history was a melancholy one. His father, whose only child he was, had been a respectable tradesman and left a good deal of property which William inherited. But before the death of his father, William had married and began in business on his own account. His guilelessness and simplicity made him the dupe of designing men and he was soon reduced to poverty along with his wife Jean (they had no children) who was every bit as innocent of worldly ways as her husband. When everything else failed, he betook himself to school-keeping – a not uncommon resource in those days for men and women who had failed.

"My connection with the school was short-lived but I remember with pleasure some things that were learned there and some peculiarities that marked Mr Selbie's teaching. As at home, so at school the Bible was almost the only lesson-book used, but our master's mode of using it was such as to make the lessons a joy rather than a labour. For example, the passage to be read was determined every day by the scholars themselves in the following way. Mr Selbie began the day's work with an extempore prayer into which he introduced several references to Scriptural or historical incidents. After prayers the pupils were asked one by one to mention anything which they had specially noted and remembered. Which of those topics was to become the lesson for that day was then decided by the votes of the scholars."

"How clever," I remarked, forgetting to keep quiet. "I don't remember you doing that with us, Father!"

Fortunately, Father was getting a little hard of hearing by

then and went straight on without comment.

"Thus on one occasion Haman and the gallows on which he was hanged happened to be chosen. So the story was read out from the book of Esther and all the pupils were led out into the playground, where Mr Selbie carefully paced off a length of fifty cubits to give some idea of the height to which the gallows was raised on which Haman was to be hanged.

"We had very little in the way of school apparatus but managed pretty well without and so we learned, like the ideal *philosophe*: 'to bore with a saw and saw with a gimblet'.

"Should't that be *gimlet*?" I whispered to Lucy. She gave me a crushing look and said, "Hush!"

"There were no costly Board Schools then, and very few school books, but plenty of good raw material," Father continued. "A born teacher contrived to turn out work every bit as good as that which now passes through the hands of these trained teachers to the approval of the government inspectors.

"My removal from Mr Selbie's school became necessary when I was little more than six years old by a sudden change in my father's circumstances. For a good many years he had been at the head of a flourishing business but about the year 1817, after the French Wars ended and brought a slump in trade, he became bankrupt and left the country to escape his creditors, after which our family never heard from him again. Of course all his effects were sold for the behoof of his creditors and my mother was left entirely penniless with three children to provide for: my eldest sister, Martha, a girl of eight; the youngest, George, a boy of two; and myself, aged six years.

My mother was obliged to leave the large house in which we had all lived and forced to move to a smaller two-roomed dwelling far from Mr Selbie's school. We had many relations in town and some of them would very gladly have helped to maintain her and her children. My mother, however, declined all direct help and, placing all her trust in Him who is Father of the fatherless and Husband to the widow, resolved to undertake the support of herself and her little ones."

"How brave of her," breathed Lucy.

"Aye, your grandmother was a woman among a thousand, active in body, shrewd in her business dealings and intelligent far beyond the usual ways of her sex: a woman that feared and loved God with a sincere and hearty devotion.

"After much consideration she opened a shop for the sale of bread and other articles that were in daily demand and, eking out her small profits by knitting and other female occupations such as spinning, which were pursued diligently in all her spare hours, she managed to provide a sufficiency of food, clothing and shelter for the whole family until such time as they were able to provide for themselves. We were neither luxuriously fed nor expensively clothed but so admirably did my mother manage that we never went in want and never came within measurable distance of cold or starvation.

"Her supreme concern was to bring us up in the nurture and admonition of the Lord. To this end, she kept up the practice of daily worship, morning and evening, set before us a shining example, strove day by day to make us acquainted with the truths and doctrines of Holy Scripture, and was specially careful to train us to the observance of the Sabbath day."

Now we understood why Father's strict emphasis on daily worship was so important to him – and why perhaps he had abandoned his profitable post of headmaster to minister to a lowly country congregation. Then he added something that none of us had known before.

"She also had a strong desire to give us the opportunity of getting as complete an education as lay within her means. In my own case, this arose from a cause which on one occasion she privately disclosed to me. Before my birth, she told me, an impression had been made upon her to the effect that the child she was to bear would be a boy and that he would become a minister of the Gospel. Of course when the first part of the expectation thus generated was fulfilled, the hope and assurance that the second part would also come to pass became all the more firmly established. Although for long the prospect of such a result was very dark and many events seemed certain to doom it to disappointment, it did at last come about, greatly to my mother's contentment."

"You and Mother must have felt just as overjoyed," ventured Lucy timidly, "when Will was elected to his professorship in Aberdeen."

"Indeed we were," said Father. "Well, after we were fairly settled down in our new abode and had grown accustomed to our reduced way of life, it was resolved I should be sent to school. But it must needs be very inexpensive. There were several such near us, some kept by broken-down men, and some by old, foolish women. Yet it had so happened that, some short time before, the obvious difficulty – the near impossibility – of obtaining a sound elementary education at trifling cost had forced itself upon the attention of several enlightened citizens, who had formed the Aberdeen Education Society and who formed the idea of opening a new school for the children of the working classes to be conducted somewhat on the lines sketched by Joseph Lancaster and at the modest fee of one penny a week for each child. A fairly suitable building in Blackfriars Street having been found and furnished, I was sent there shortly after its opening. At that time it was attended, as well as I can guess, by some three hundred boys."

"What about the girls?" I asked rather daringly.

"The Society shortly established a similar girls' school in Harriet Street. None of the pupils were by any means of the very poorest class; in fact most of them were decently clad, the sons of working men, mechanics and the like, who were in fairly comfortable circumstances, without having much to spare. The gentleman who was at the head of it in my day was college-bred and, although not perhaps an accomplished scholar, surpassed all the men I have ever known as a teacher and a manager of boys. He was also a good musician and at all odd and otherwise unemployed moments the boys were practised in the singing of psalm tunes."

"But you haven't told us his name," Lucy said. This was in fact a well-worn family joke.

"I do believe it escapes my memory, Lucy dear. Perhaps it was Ramsbotten or Rawsthorne. No, I have it!" exclaimed Father triumphantly. "Robertson! Peter Robertson was his name and his daughter, Jane, was . . . er . . ."

"Mother!" we both shouted.

"Yes, of course. I had quite forgot. Well, as the school occupied two floors, a second and subordinate master was required but he was a younger man, pursuing his own studies with a view to the ministry, and was there merely as a stopgap until the Society should be able to find more suitable premises with room for the whole school in one great hall and under a single master. The pupils were divided into nine classes, each of some thirty-five boys, and placed accordingly to the mastery which they had attained to in the art of reading and spelling.

"In the first class the scholars were taught the alphabet, learning to know the letters by writing them with their index finger in sand spread on a desk prepared for the purpose, with an appliance for smoothing the sand after each attempt. The boys in the ninth class were able to read with fluency and able also to spell fairly well. All the teaching of the first eight classes was carried out by boys selected for the purpose from the ninth class, their pupils being drafted into sections of eight or nine boys ranged in a circle round a large card on which was pasted a portion of text usually taken from the Bible. This was read and reread so often during the allotted time that any boy of tolerable smartness might have been able to repeat the whole lesson from memory. The cards were changed every day.

"The monitors received separate instruction – at least occasionally. They were also privileged to read from books – some of the anthologies of those days containing, amongst other things, pieces such as *John Gilpin* or *Boniface and Aimwell* together with bits from the *Spectator* and such like."

"*Boniface* and who?" I asked, having now taken over the secretarial task from Lucy.

"*Aimwell*, my dear. *Boniface* and *Aimwell* are characters from *The Beaux' Stratagem*, a Restoration play and hardly a suitable piece to be read by young ladies such as yourselves. But we young lads thought it great fun in those days. And it hardly needs to be said that when the monitors were thus employed under the supervision of one of themselves there was a good deal of idle chatter.

"I joined the school when the principal master (your late grandfather) was absent. His substitute put me into the eighth class but after Mr Robertson's return a few days later I was transferred to the highest or ninth class, in which I continued for the space of nearly seven years. Of course as far as reading was concerned I learned nothing from my schoolwork although I daresay the daily intercourse with boys of all sorts and conditions added not a little to my knowledge of life, of persons and of things.

"When I say I learned nothing I really mean that next to nothing was done to explain what we were reading. It was all more or less reading and spelling by rote: nothing more. That was the hallmark of the Lancastrian system so popular in those days. What came many years later to be called intellectual teaching had not then been introduced anywhere and the boys taught by the monitorial system proved quite able to hold their own against all others in the business of life. Many of them turned out very well indeed. I suppose the mere fact that they were rigorously trained to habits of punctuality and self-control by being entrusted with the care of other boys told in their favour.

"As they had to teach the younger children repetitively, the little that they knew came to be known very thoroughly. In course of time our master began to teach English Grammar and a little Geography to the more advanced pupils. This was done at a separate hour set apart for the purpose and must have been a heavy tax on the little leisure left to your grandfather. Writing on slate was taught over the whole school; writing upon paper only to boys in the higher classes during an hour every morning. By that I certainly benefited although I never became an accomplished penman."

"We know that only too well," I muttered, "That's why we're doing all this work". But neither of us truly minded: we enjoyed hearing those tales about old-fashioned ways of teaching.

"Arithmetic," Father went on methodically, "was well and carefully taught – but here, in addition to the monitorial lessons that came in the regular course, an evening class was formed, for attendance at which a fee was charged and the more advanced boys practised at a separate desk while the others were engaged with their reading and spelling lessons. In the simple and compound rules of proportion and practice, and to some extent in vulgar and decimal fractions, we senior boys became very proficient. And among those more able pupils I very soon came to hold the first place. Indeed I never had any difficulty with arithmetic but I came very much to regret that no pain was taken to make me acquainted with the arithmetical principles on which the rules were based.

"When visitors came to the school an exhibition or demonstration was usually made of our skills – always in arithmetic and sometimes also in writing and spelling. This was sure to call forth expressions of admiration from our audience. And when the school moved to its new building the occasion was notable for the holding of a public exhibition, by which the Directors of the Society hoped both to excite the public interest in their undertaking and to raise money towards the expense of the new building. The exhibition of the boys and their various exercises was to be in a public hall, to which admission was to be by tickets sufficiently expensive to ensure a somewhat select audience. A picked group of us, I guess thirty or forty, was marched to the hall and in the presence of a large number of ladies and gentlemen were put through the various evolutions in which we were thoroughly practised at school in order to demonstrate our prowess in reading, writing and arithmetic.

"The master (your grandfather, my dears) told us beforehand that the audience, if pleased with us, would stamp their feet or, as he called it, "ruff". If displeased, they would hiss. There was certainly no hissing. I have no idea what the pecuniary result was but certainly the school rose at once to a high place in public esteem and the number of scholars increased greatly. In the new building there was far greater convenience and as we were now under one roof and in one room the master was able, with the assistance of the monitors, to superintend the whole business of teaching several hundred boys. One selected boy, known as the 'general monitor', had oversight of the other monitors as well as of the whole school. This position became mine soon after entering the ninth class and remained so until I left the school."

By this time, both Lucy and I were exhausted and Father himself seemed to feel he had reached a natural break in his history. We began again some days later with a tale that he had never told us before.

* * * *

"We had very few school holidays in those days. At Christmas we got a single week and at midsummer three or at most later four weeks. During the summer holidays I generally visited friends in the country and it was on one of those visits that an incident occurred which, insignificant as it was, made an impression on my mind which has never been effaced by all the experiences of a long life.

"I had been given the loan of a clasp knife from the man with whom I was staying and it was obviously a favourite of his, being kept locked away always in a private cupboard. But while using it I had the misfortune to break the pin on which the blade turned.

"What was to be done? I could not possibly offer it back in its broken condition and I had not courage enough to confess what had happened. Instead I carried it to the blacksmith who lived about a mile away and asked him to mend it. He could not do it straight away but promised it should be done in a day or two. Of course the work had to be paid for and I had no money, not even the smallest coin. In fact I never had any in those days.

"By the time I got home there was a message asking me to

go to the house of another acquaintance (a general merchant) some miles off and to stay there for a few days. While there, a boy came to his shop asking for a ha-pennyworth of marbles. My friend the shopkeeper happened to have none, but I had a pocketful which I had brought from town and so offered to supply the lad. Thus I became possessed of a ha-penny which, as it turned out, was exactly the charge made by the blacksmith for mending the knife. I daresay most people will be disposed to laugh at this incident but to me it was a clear instance of an all-guiding Providence."

I sat thinking solemnly of all my own carelessness in losing or breaking my possessions. How fortunate we were compared to Father in his youth!

"While on this subject," said Father after a few moments' deliberation, "I may as well describe another singular incident in my boyish experience. An old school friend had made an electrical machine and he and I both took it one winter's evening to our schoolmaster's house, some miles out of town. We continued our experiments till much past my usual time of going home and I knew I would be blamed for staying out so late. Eventually I made my way alone through the deserted streets, by no means relishing the experience, for in those days we boys all had an awful dread of being picked up by the young medicals to be converted into subjects for dissection."

Lucy and I both shuddered at the horrible thoughts that this conjured up but said nothing.

"However, go I must and run the risk. Leaving the master's house I earnestly committed myself in prayer to the care and keeping of God and, strange to relate, no sooner was I outside than a man carrying a lighted lantern came along. I kept close by his side and it turned out that his way lay with mine until I was within a few yards of my mother's door. Perhaps most people could report such so-called coincidences but to me it was a stimulus to daily prayer and all along I have tried to carry into practice the saying, 'In all thy ways acknowledge God, and He will guide thy steps'.

"Having now reached my fourteenth year, I was thoroughly tired of school where I was learning nothing but merely spent the long day superintending the other boys. I wanted either to be acquiring knowledge or finding work so that I could assist my mother. So, towards the end of the year 1824, I was taken on trial by a druggist with the view to an apprenticeship.

"I had been there for no more than a few weeks when my old schoolmaster, Mr Robertson . . ."

"Our grandfather Peter!" we chorused

"As I said," Father repeated with a censorious glare, "Mr Robertson sought me out and persuaded my mother to send me back to school. 'Your son,' said he, 'is capable of better things and the Society has patrons who will readily find young William a more suitable situation.' So I returned to school and sure enough several berths were proposed – clerkships and the like – all of which I declined. In the summer of 1825 I finally left and spent several months with a market gardener until the cold weather began to be injurious to my health and an acquaintance who was in business as a wood-turner proved willing to take me on as an apprentice. Thereupon I was handed over to his care and entered into a bargain to serve an apprenticeship of five years."

"So that's how you were able to make the spinning-top for me at Elgin," exclaimed Lucy.

"Indeed, my dear, I soon became somewhat skilled in the use of a lathe but my strength was hardly enough for some of the harder tasks that had to be done. My master never knowingly overtaxed me, yet I took great pride in doing my utmost for his benefit. He was a most able man of good

179

intelligence and since the two of us were alone in the shop we held many serious conversations from which I learned much more than wood-turning.

"I had always been fond of books, reading everything that came my way, though in truth there was not much leisure time, work hours extending from six o'clock in the morning till eight at night; but during the winter months we could not start work until daylight and I made full use of this free time, reading all the way to and from home and also whenever I had a message to take from one part of the town to another. In those days I was fond of poetry and the first book I bought with money of my own was a copy of Milton's *Paradise Lost*. I used also to do a good deal in the way of rhyming and found that I could indulge this idle art while busy at work."

I was fascinated by this new information and said, "Do you still have any of that poetry, Father?"

"Whatever I composed then has long ago disappeared and nobody is the poorer," he answered tersely. "In any case I could keep a hundred or so lines in my head at a time and had little need to write them down. Now we must go on. Don't interrupt, my child.

"When the time of my apprenticeship came to an end, I worked as a journeyman for about eighteen months but during a great part of that time I was busy at all spare moments picking up knowledge – at first without any ulterior object. I was led, like the blind, by a way I knew not . . ."

"That's from Isaiah," I whispered.

". . . but that way," continued Father, levelling his white eyebrows at me with disapproval, "led quite unexpectedly to my entering College in the session of 1832-33 – and I now proceed to give an account of the steps whereby this end was at length attained."

Lucy, who was writing, could hardly stifle a yawn and Father announced: "We shall continue our tale the morn."

* * * *

Now it was my turn to be amanuensis when we sat down the following evening. The rain battered on the window panes and I was glad to be settled at such a pleasant task.

"One evening in the summer of 1831," began Father, "I made a call upon my cousin, John Michie, at his shop in the Netherkirkgate of Aberdeen. His shop occupied that rounded corner known as Wallace's Neuk which separates the Netherkirkgate from Carnegie's Brae. John lived in Woodside and was a tinsmith of some repute, so his shop was a frequent place of resort for respectable young men, many being engaged in the laudable work of Sabbath School teaching. One of the lads there, Roy by name, had been a school-fellow of mine and knew that I possessed some Latin books which had come to me as school prizes some years before; he knew also that I had never used them.

"It came out in the course of our talk that Roy had determined to begin the study of Latin with the view of qualifying for one of the learned professions and he asked me whether I might be disposed to sell him such books as I had. I was ill-prepared to give him a definite answer there and then but said I would consider the matter and let him know the result in a day or two.

"As soon as I got home, the books were hunted out and examined with great care; and I thought to myself, why should I not learn Latin myself? I was then twenty years old, had served an apprenticeship to the craft of a turner, was working as a journeyman, and had until then no other ambition consciously in my mind. I had chosen my own way in life, contrary to all the wishes of my friends, who had all destined me to a life of study, and my knowledge of this may have slowly been exercising an influence upon me.

"Anyway, the decision I came to was to keep the books and learn from them what I could. They were exactly the kind of books a beginner wanted, having been chosen, seven years before, by your grandfather for the very reason. They comprised Ruddiman's *Rudiments*, the *Colloquies* of Corderius, and the *History* of Cornelius Nepos. In addition to these, I had an old copy of Caesar's *De Bello Gallico*, which I had picked up for two pence, together with a Young's Latin-English and English-Latin Dictionary, which by some chance or another was found among the volumes that formed the family library.

"This was a turning point in my life. Having once made up my mind, I set to work without delay and with all my heart. There was not much spare time at my disposal. The work on which my daily bread depended occupied me from six in the morning till eight at night, with intervals of one hour each for breakfast and dinner; and in those days there were neither holidays nor half holidays. The work hours on Saturday were as many as on Monday or Tuesday. New Year's Day and the two Sacramental Fast-days in April and October were the only free days during the year. My memory was pretty good and a considerable part of what had to be learned by heart I was able to pick up on my way to and from work.

"I began of course with the rudiments. Ruddiman's book . . ."

"Whoever was Ruddiman?" I asked.

"Thomas Ruddiman," said Father solemnly, "was a farmer's son from Boyndie in Banffshire. He ran away from home at sixteen, was robbed by highwaymen on his way to Aberdeen but won a bursary to study classics at King's College. He gained his M.A. there and then went to

Edinburgh where he was employed in the Advocates' Library. In 1714 or thereabouts he published his *Rudiments of the Latin Tongue*."

"How funny. Ruddiman's *Rudiments!*"

"A most important book, Alice, and a most eminent scholar. He became chief librarian of the Advocate's Library. Anyway, his Latin primer was written in the form of Question and Answer, and in two columns – the one in Latin, the other in English. As I knew no better, I learned both columns by heart and in that way gathered a considerable vocabulary.

"Twas, I believe, no hardship or disadvantage that I had to work with my hands from morning to night. I could easily turn the day's lesson over in my mind while turning the lathe – with the result was that every lesson was thoroughly mastered.

"For acquiring the rules of Latin syntax, a few weeks sufficed and then I began the *Colloquies* of Corderius – he taught Latin to Calvin in Geneva – but I found his work dry, so I laid the book aside and took Cornelius Nepos instead. This proved more interesting and challenging. It may seem strange, Alice, but all my life I have never much enjoyed easy tasks, preferring to tackle difficult problems and to work those out for myself without assistance from others."

"I know that, Father. That's why you always say to us, 'Get on. Do it for yourself.'"

"Indeed. It is owing to my mental constitution in this regard that I have had the satisfaction of overcoming difficulties unaided throughout my life. At any rate, by the time I had read through Nepos, I had picked up an acquaintance with the histories of Greece and Rome, together with something of Classical geography. So I then took up Caesar's *Commentaries* and found that work so easy that I contented myself with reading the first and

second Books of his *Gallic War*. It was now the beginning
of the year 1832 and meantime a copy of Virgil had come
into my hands. This was my first introduction to Latin
poetry and it seemed so hard a nut to crack that on this
occasion I began to look about for help and direction.
Someone told me of an evening school kept by a man who
was believed to be a Latin scholar and I went therefore and
offered myself as a pupil anxious to learn Latin. He readily
agreed to teach me but as soon as I produced my Virgil, he
shook his head and confessed his inability to help me.

"What was I to do now? It so happened that a friend of
mine, a workman like myself, had a brother who was a
student under Dr Melvin at the town's Grammar School.
Until now I had told no one of my studies but in my
necessity I made a confidant of this young man and he
brought me to his brother, David Craig, who initiated me
into the mysteries of hexameter verse and advised me to lay
aside Virgil for the present and to take up Ovid's
Metamorphoses instead and to supply myself also with a
copy of Melvin's *Grammar*.

"I read enough of Ovid to introduce me to Greek
mythology. Melvin's *Grammar* contained rules in Latin
verse for determining the gender of nouns and the mode of
their declension, together with the conjugation of verbs and
the quantities of all the vowels. All these I learned
thoroughly by heart and found them of the greatest possible
use in my studies. By and by I was able to read the first
book of the *Aeneid*; then I took up Horace, finding this so
interesting that I committed to memory all the Odes.
Meantime I had been writing so-called versions – these were
pieces of English composed by Dr Melvin for the purpose of
being turned into Latin prose by his pupils in the fourth and
fifth classes of the Grammar School and so contrived as to
illustrate all the peculiarities of Latin construction.

"David Craig constantly encouraged me, saying he thought I should go further and consider entering College. Each of the town's two Colleges, King's in Old Aberdeen and Marischal, had a number of bursaries which were awarded at the start of every session. David suggested I might try for a bursary at King's at the end of October.

"It was then near the end of September and instant decision was required. There was only one person who I felt I could safely ask for advice – yes, my old schoolmaster and your grandfather, Mr Peter Robertson – and to him I accordingly went. Once he had heard me out, he was both surprised and pleased, for he had never been greatly satisfied with my resolution to learn a trade. Not that he had ever encouraged me to study for one of the learned professions – on the contrary he had thrown cold water on such a proposition when six years or so before I had suggested it, after obtaining from him as prizes the volumes already mentioned. No, he would have had me become a clerk or an accountant and as you know had procured me more than one offer of that kind.

"Now the case was wholly altered and he advised that I should pursue my aims, though he saw no hope of success for me at the bursary competition after only fifteen months' private study. However, he gave me a letter of introduction to the headmaster of the Old Town Grammar School and I was enrolled as a pupil there just three weeks before the day on which the competition was fixed to start.

"That's enough for today, Alice. Lucy can take over tomorrow – no, it's the Sabbath the morn. I must away and prepare my sermon."

"Thank goodness," breathed Lucy in my ear, "for the day of rest!"

* * * *

185

"At the Grammar School," began Father on the Monday without preamble, "I read Livy and wrote more 'versions' from Gibbon's *Decline and Fall of the Roman Empire*. These required some ingenuity before they could be rendered into Latin. But the greatest benefit came from social intercourse with my fellow scholars, most of whom were to be my fellow competitors for bursaries and eventually fellow students at college.

"At length the day of the Competition arrived. It fell upon the Monday before the last day in October and lasted to the following day. The Bursary Competition in those days was, and indeed still is, a great event. At King's College, two days were spent on the work, at Marischal College only one. At the former, the candidates had to translate English into Latin and Latin into English; at the latter only English into Latin. At Marischal, the candidates for the most part belonged to Aberdeen and had been educated at the Grammar school there. Most were young and not a few mere boys. Their exercises were examined and valued the same night and the results known the following morning. Many of the competitors in fact sat up all night and hung around the College until they learned their fate.

"At King's College, however, the competitors were gathered from many different parishes, some at a great distance. They were of varying ages, from fifteen or sixteen up to thirty or forty years of age. Some had been employed as schoolmasters in the Highlands or Islands; others, like myself, had been employed in labour of various kinds. Moreover the results of the competition were not made known until at least midday on the Wednesday. Early on the Monday morning therefore I made my way in some trepidation to Old Aberdeen and joined the anxious group of nearly two hundred who were assembled in the College quadrangle.

"In due course we were called into the hall and there arranged at long tables. Then one of the professors dictated a piece of English, taken, as it happened, from Gibbon, and this we were directed to turn into Latin as best we could. No limit was set to the time in which the exercise might be finished and when dusk came on lighted candles were brought in, some of the competitors remaining at their task until the evening was well advanced. Those of course were persons who, notwithstanding their dogged perseverance, had no chance of success. For myself, I was done early, but instead of giving up my exercise at once as I ought to have done, I sat there and went over it again and again, eventually altering the construction of one sentence, making a change which necessitated other alterations, with the result that I left one of the verbs unchanged and therefore wrong.

"When I came out, a number of the men were standing around in the quad and of course I was closely examined about the way I had tackled this or that sentence; then, horror of horrors, it dawned on me that I had committed the awful blunder described. I made no attempt to hide the truth and soon saw that my error was in a high degree agreeable to some of my questioners, who assumed that my chance of success was completely gone. I went home not only crestfallen but in the deepest despair – for to me, a penniless lad and the son of a widow, success was a matter almost of life or death. I gathered all my exercise books together, went out into the fields, tore them to shreds and scattered these to the four winds.

"For all that, I made my way next morning to the examination hall to perform the work of the day as best I could, then waited as patiently as possible for the declaration of the result on the following day, Wednesday. On that day there were many anxious faces for far fewer bursaries were available than there are now and all of them were of less

value, varying from something like £3 to about £20. The
names of the successful competitors were called out in order
of merit. At length, after thirteen or fourteen had been
announced, my name was called. Trembling all over I went
forward and found that a bursary of £10 had been awarded
me. I was more than content and went immediately with the
son of one of the professors and bought a second hand copy
of Moore's *Greek Grammar* before going home to carry the
good news to my mother."

"How old were you by then?" we asked Father, thinking
how young Will and George had been when they went to
university.

"When I entered College in 1832, I was already in the
twenty-second year of my age. Even so, a good many were
still older. My knowledge was of course woefully deficient
for I knew nothing of Greek, not even the alphabet.
Besides, I had mixed so little with persons of any social
standing that I knew little of how I should conduct myself in
the society to which I was now introduced. I was shy and
timid but, I hope, also modest and unpretending. Yet I was
kindly received by my new associates and soon felt quite at
ease.

"To be sure, I was not much among them for my home
was in the town of Aberdeen while most of the students had
lodgings in the Old Town, so I mixed with them only during
classes and for the short periods before and after class hours
spent in walking about the college quad or under the old
piazza. On the same day that my attendance at College
began, I started as a tutor in the family of a friend at a small
fee – which however was as great as a mere beginner had
any right to expect – and I also found employment for an
hour a day in what was at that time the best English school
in town – yes, twas the West End Academy! Besides
compelling me to pay some attention to my dress and

deportment, these engagements served to introduce me to better paying employment in private tuition, a work in which I mostly depended for a living during the greater part of my undergraduate course.

"At the same time they caused a good deal of interruption to my college studies, especially after I got into so much work as to occupy five or six hours a day, which came to be the case after the close of my first session. During my first session, however, I felt no inconvenience. What little classwork had to be done was easy and could mostly be accomplished on the way to and from College, the distance I had to walk, about eight miles a day, giving me sufficient exercise for the purpose of health.

"That first session we had nothing to attend to but Latin and Greek. The Greek class, was taught by a Dr Macpherson – a medical man I believe, quite elderly and a very poor scholar, though quite a gentleman. The teaching was entirely mechanical. We had no information about the accents or the syntax, nor about the Greek authors or the Greek people. There was nothing to make us think, nothing to stir us to inquiry or tempt us to study for ourselves. Most persons nowadays go to College with more knowledge of the language and the culture of Greece than we were masters of when the session came to an end. It cannot be said that Dr Macpherson was respected by the students. He was often welcomed into the College quadrangle with, 'Three cheers for the Chieftain of Eigg!' In his classroom, peas were shot about plentifully and when one chanced to hit him he would remark, 'That was well aimed'.

"He was Vice-Principal of the University and it was commonly said that, when he succeeded to that office, his first words at home were, 'Thank God I won't have to say the prayer again' – meaning the morning prayer which at that time was given in College by the Regents in turn, each for a week at a time.

"Our other professor during the first year was Dr Forbes, a clergyman and a junior minister of the parish in which the College stood. He was Professor of Latin and also of Chemistry – a somewhat remarkable conjunction of offices – and very different in character from Dr Macpherson. He kept good order but it cannot be said that his teaching was much superior to that of his colleague. In the Latin class he was nicknamed 'Prosody', from the amount of attention which he bestowed upon the metres of Horace. When Dr Forbes lectured, he enjoyed offering us moral reflections and giving us advice about our conduct in life: the only true way to happiness, he said, was summed up in Horace's maxim, *nil admirari*."

"Does that mean 'Don't expect to be admired by anyone'?" ventured Lucy. She had made little of Latin.

Father sighed testily: "Of course it does not, Lucy. Tell her, Alice."

"Er . . . it means, 'Be amazed by nothing.'" I liked Horace myself.

"When Forbes drew an inference from anything he said it was always introduced by the words, 'Hence; therefore, consequently . . . ' We chuckled much over this practice privately but in class nobody ventured to take any liberties. I am sure he put me down for a blockhead at the start but after he had put me through a long train of questions, selecting all the most difficult examples that came to his head, I believe I became a favourite of his.

"When the session was half over, there began to be a good deal of talk about prizes. Up to this time these had been allotted by the votes of the members from each class and there had been, as I learned, much canvassing for votes and not a little bribery in the way of treating. Now, for the first time, the prizes were to be determined by competition at the end of the session. For me, as one who did not live in the midst of the students and had no means of ingratiating myself, the change was welcome for it gave a fair chance of competing simply on the grounds of scholarship. Under the new plan even those who perhaps never had an opportunity to shine in the presence of the class, who perhaps had seldom been called up for examination, had it in their power to show what was in them and to make it plain whether they had profited by the class teaching.

"The first examination was for the Latin class attended by the first year students. I went into it with fear and trembling, not because I was unprepared but simply from my constitutional nervousness and the novelty of the position for someone with my lack of experience. The time allowed for the test paper was limited and as the time drew to an end my hand trembled so much that the words were written in great straggling, almost illegible letters. Besides that, when I dried my paper at the fire, I was foolish enough to let it become discoloured by the heat. Of course I assumed that my chance of distinction had come to an end. But not so.

"Next came the examination in Greek. To this I went in a most self-possessed condition: I was firm as a rock, determined to do my best and not to yield to my natural impetuosity in the one hand, nor to nervousness on the other. I went on composedly from beginning to end of the paper and came away satisfied that however long I might have taken the thing was as well done as I could have hoped.

"The result was not to be announced till the breaking-up day and meantime the anxiety was intense. Then we in the first Greek class were informed that our Latin examination had been set aside because it had been judged that many of the students had copied from one another or had used cribs. The Senatus had therefore resolved to make a new trial. All students who wished were asked to submit to a *viva voce* examination to be held immediately on the rising of the

Greek class. Twelve aspirants came forward. I was one of them and we were ushered into a private room from which, one by one, we were called into the Senate Room and examined on passages from Livy and Horace. All I can remember is that in reading a line in Horace the work *inopes* occurred and I pronounced the short *o* long. After translating the portions assigned I was asked to scan the line and did so correctly. The examiners then asked if I had at first read the line right. Of course I had by this time noticed my error and answered accordingly.

"Next day the prizes were distributed and I was awarded the first prize in Latin and the first in Greek. This place in the class I kept to the end of the curriculum for, although I did not in the second year hold so high a place in the prize list, I regained my original place in the third year and kept it in the fourth year, gaining also the Hutton prize which at that time was the only special distinction which the University had to bestow.

"That's enough," announced Father, somewhat to our relief. "Tomorrow we will go on."

But he never did!

EPILOGUE

The Dear Auld Hame

Oh, the auld hame, the dear auld hame!
Close by the kirk it stood;
Wi' ne'er anither hoose in sicht,
Embowered in a wood.
White roses twined the windows roon,
While ivy decked the waa;
An' o'er the door sweet briar we trained –
Fu' weel I min' it aa.

An ample yaird, weel stocked wi' flooers,
Shrub, berry-buss an' tree.
Lay roun' the hoose on ivery side,
A picture fair tae see.
There ilk ane had an aipple tree,
Ilk ane a garden plot
Where grew sweet pinks an' violets
An' blue forget-me-not.

Twas fair, sae fair i' the bonnie spring
When leaves were buddin' green,
The aipple decked wi' clusters rare
Wi' bridal white the gean.
The beech hedge cast his auld broon coat –
Had keepit the frost awa' –
An' trigged him in a bran' new suit,
A wunner tae ane an aa.

195

Oor lessons dane, we roamed the wuids,
Wi' sangs a merry band
The firstlin' o each flooer we laid
Wi' pride in Mither's hand.
An' whiles in quest o a sair-socht nest
We gaed ower far astray;
But helter-skelter hame we raced
At Faither's first "Coo-ee!"

In simmer's pride twas fairer still,
Wi' mony a sheltered nook,
Where aft we sat in the leafy shade
Wi' work or story book.
At twilicht's hush, blackbird an' thrush
Wi' music filled the air –
Ah me! I hear nae sangs like these
Sin' last I heard them there.

Maybe the birds aye sing as sweet
As braw may bloom the flooers;
Maybe, maybe, but och, they bloom
For ither hauns than oors.
Nae mair the dear wuids echo back
Oor lauchter an' oor sang;
Nor rings the hoose wi' merry din
Whan winter nichts are lang.

A stranger stauns in Faither's place –
We hear his voice nae mair –
Sae maisterfu' his pulpit word,
Sae earnest in his prayer –
For he's wan safe tae his far, far hame
An five o' us beside;
The circle's dwinin' narra' noo
That eesed tae be sae wide.

Ah yes! Oor love may well haud oot the cauld
As England's poet said.
Yet canna snatch oor dear anes frae
The cauld, cauld grip o' daith.
But a Love that's higher, wiser far
Than the best oor hairts provide
Will herd them safe until we be
At hame the tither side.

We're aa grown up an' scattered noo
Far frae the dear auld hame;
An' some hae fand an honoured place
An won a famous name;
But heich or low, in foreign lands,
Or here, or onywhere,
Nane o's will e'er forgot oor hame
Or aa we lairned there.

Nellie Allan Smith

ALICE: A POSTSCRIPT

Following their marriage in 1881, Alice and Hans went to live in Bernberg-on-Saale in eastern Germany, where Hans, with financial help from his brother-in-law Will, set up an ironmonger's business. That venture proved a failure, however, as did every other of his attempts to become a successful businessman in Berlin and Königsberg. Eventually, the couple settled in Braunschweig where Hans worked, I assume, as an auditor in the civil service, a post that provided greater stability for Alice and her growing family.

Hans and Alice had five children: Jeannie, Lucy, William, Alfred and Kurt. Both girls became teachers. Jeannie inherited the family aptitude for maths and taught at a Gymnasium in Aachen, while Lucy taught domestic science in Braunschweig. William became a quartermaster, Alfred a missionary and Kurt a local government administrator.

Alice seems to have visited Scotland frequently during the early years of her marriage and no doubt it was Will who met the travel costs. Those visits inevitably ended with the onset of World War I and the consequent separation from her roots in Scotland must have proved very hard for Alice. The three sons naturally had to serve in the German armed forces from 1914 to 1918 and living conditions became very harsh indeed towards the end of the war. She describes in her memoirs of that later period how ashamed she was of having to spend her day constantly scrounging for food and fuel.

All the family survived the war, however. The three sons soon married but the two daughters remained unmarried throughout their lives. In due course Hans retired;

grandchildren arrived and eventually it was Lucy who bought a house for her parents in Braunschweig, just as Will had done in Aberdeen forty years previously. There the three lived, Lucy, Hans and Alice. Hans died in 1939.

Alice must always have been the dominant figure in the marriage. She had, I am certain, quickly realised her husband's limitations in terms of business sense and so became the stronger partner. The bond between herself and her five children was always a powerful one – possibly too intense – and in turn they always put their mother at the forefront of their affections, sometimes (in the case of the sons) at the expense of their wives.

In the end Alice was spared the final disasters and indignities of World War II, dying peacefully in June, 1943, at the age of 85. Lucy, Jeannie, Alfred and his wife lived together in the Braunschweig house until their eventual deaths.

A.H.

WILLIAM ROBERTSON SMITH AND
THE HISTORICAL CONTEXT

Three Scotsmen of genius from the late Victorian period
have a permanent niche in history, both nationally and
internationally, and all share the common fortune of being as
well known by their initials as by their full names. Each
knew one another, though not intimately, and while all died
tragically young, each made a significant yet very different
contribution to our Scottish and international heritage.

Of these three, the poet and novelist Robert Louis
Stevenson (RLS) is perhaps the most familiar to everyone.
James Clerk Maxwell (JCM) made fundamental and far-
reaching discoveries concerning atomic theory and the
electro-magnetic spectrum, with repercussions for modern
physics and technology that now affect every aspect of our
daily lives. William Robertson Smith (WRS) is probably the
least widely known, except among anthropologists and
theologians, yet he revolutionised our understanding of
religion and introduced seminal concepts about the nature of
group relationships which Sigmund Freud, amongst many
others, was later to acknowledge as basic to his own theories
of the unconscious mind.

In her memoirs, Alice has described her eldest brother's
much humbler origins than those of Stevenson or Maxwell.
She tells also how, while a theological student in Edinburgh,
WRS became assistant to Peter Guthrie Tait, close friend of
both James Clerk Maxwell and William Thomson, later Lord
Kelvin. Tait held the chair of Natural Philosophy (Physics)
at Edinburgh University and had been deeply impressed by
the young Robertson Smith's scientific and mathematical
skills. At the British Association for the Advancement of

Science in 1871, he was to introduce WRS into the company of internationally renowned scientists such as Heinrich Helmholtz and Thomas Huxley, as well as to Thomas Spencer Baynes who had been appointed editor of the forthcoming ninth edition of the *Encyclopaedia Britannica*, published between 1875 and 1888 by the Edinburgh firm of Messrs A. & C. Black. Huxley and Clerk Maxwell were already scientific advisers to the project.

Those contacts led to an invitation being extended to WRS to write some of the biblical articles for the encyclopaedia, the first of those appearing in Volume II [ANG-ATH] at the end of 1875, with items on "Angel" and "Ark of the Covenant". It was the subsequent volume, however, published that same year and containing WRS's article "Bible" which provoked an immediate outcry amongst the Scottish clergy. Smith was arraigned before the General Assembly of the Free Church and eventually subjected to a trial for heresy on a number of counts, chief of which related to his attribution of the book of Deuteronomy to a date centuries after the death of its assumed author, Moses. WRS had been by no means the first to question Mosaic authorship but Smith's academic status and the open publication of such an idea within an encyclopaedia likely to be perused by the man in the street was thought scandalous.

Smith's acute forensic skills were sufficiently brilliant to save him from actual conviction by the Assembly but a year later the Free Kirk resorted to the rather shameful alternative of dismissing him outright from his chair at Aberdeen. He then moved to Edinburgh, becoming assistant editor of the *Encyclopaedia Britannica* under Baynes and ultimately chief editor, seeing the enormous project through to its completion in 1888. WRS had, meantime, been appointed Reader in Arabic at Trinity College, Cambridge, where his influence led the young James G. Frazer to the study of anthropology and ultimately to the compilation of that immense work, *The Sacred Bough*. Smith himself went on to become University Librarian at Cambridge and subsequently Adams Professor of Arabic there before dying of spinal tuberculosis in 1894 at the age of 47. His writings on the origins of religion – in particular *The Religion of the Semites* – remain key texts for students of anthropology and comparative religion.

While William Robertson Smith was without question the most illustrious member of his family, his parents, brothers and sisters shared many of his attributes, interests and talents. His younger brother, George, who died tragically of tuberculosis at the age of 18, was reputed to be fully as intellectually able as WRS himself. The third brother, Charles, became Professor of Physics and Mathematics in Madras and subsequently Director of Madras Observatory. The girls of the family were necessarily excluded from such academic pursuits but led lives which are of historical and cultural interest in their own right.

Alice's memoirs are simple, sincere and unadorned – she herself simply called them "Chats to my grandchildren". They illustrate in particular the virtually insuperable barriers against parity of educational opportunity for girls during the Victorian era but they also give a remarkably vivid picture of how the family conducted their lives as children of the manse within a relatively isolated Aberdeenshire Free Church parish. The guiding and controlling influence of the eldest brother, William Robertson Smith, is everywhere apparent, yet Alice's individuality and feelings shine through very clearly indeed.

G.K.B.